# LAMP OF ETERNAL LIGHTS

### THE BIOGRAPHY OF SAINT CHARBEL MAKHLOUF (1828-1898)

BY

*ELIAS TURK*

**Imprimatur**

Lebanon - Zahle
08 September 2016

**ARCHBISHOP ISSAM JOHN DARWISH**

MELKITE GREEK CATHOLIC ARCHBISHOP
OF FURZOL, ZAHLE AND THE BEKAA

*To my father and mother
who taught me to pray to God
and ask for the intercession of his saints*

Copyright © 2016 by Elias Turk.
All rights reserved.

Subscribe on Elias Turk's
YouTube channel:
*A Catholic in Rome*

**Editing and proofreading:**
Fr. Geoffrey Abdallah

**Cover Design by:**
OUBA'S PRINT HOUSE.
Lebanon-Zahle, Hoch El Omara.
Tel. +961 8 814458      Cell. +961 3 824458
Site: www.jojouba.com
e-mail: georges@jojouba.com

**Cover Image:** Saint Charbel's photo. Saint Charbel's shrine.
Saint Maroun's monastery- Annaya, Lebanon.

## *Preface*

When I first thought of writing this book, I asked God for the grace to be able to do it. But I think I was granted much more than just a possibility to look into Saint Charbel's astonishing life. What started as simply writing Saint Charbel's biography eventually resulted in me becoming very familiar with the Saint. His great life was engraved upon my heart, soul and imagination.

I thought I knew enough about this Saint, being a Christian Lebanese who had the opportunity to visit his shrine and hear his story many times. However, we can never truly understand the great mysteries of a human life, especially those who become saints. The days I spent researching this book and visiting his native village Bekaakafra, and his shrine in Annaya, became much more than just an academic quest to understand and write about his fascinating life.

As a Saint, Charbel Makhlouf is now living the extraordinary joy of heaven. As it is said in Saint Alphonsus De Liguori's book *Preparation for Death*, a book particularly precious to the Saint: «O ye saints! who for the love of that God who you loved alone, upon this earth, knew how to mortify your bodies; and now your relics are kept and prized as sacred relics in golden shrines; and your souls which are beatified, rejoice in the presence of God, waiting for the final Day, when your bodies even, will again become the companions of your souls in glory, as they were the companions of your souls in bearing the cross of this world»[1].

The Christian's testimony of sainthood is not made to fascinate human beings but to inspire them in moving forward. The testimony of a saint is a wakeup call for us to embrace God's call just like the saints did. I pray to the merciful God to transform you, dear readers, into true friends of Saint Charbel. Lastly, I ask Saint Charbel to quench the thirst in the heart of many believers, wishing to know him better.

Lebanon, Zahle
16th July 2016
The vigil of Saint Charbel's Feast Day.
**Elias Turk**

---

[1] A. DE LIGUORI, *Preparation for Death*, J.B. Lippincott and co., England-London 1869, Consideration I, second point, p. 4.

# INTRODUCTION

Very often during winter, storms occur. Huge clouds gather to create a spectacular show of lights and sounds, known as lightning and thunder. A show that is astonishing yet petrifying at the same time. Lights unleash from the sky to invade the land or to remain at high altitudes. Thunder strikes: very deep sounds, capable of showing our nothingness in front of the greatness of our Creator. Lights and sounds that open up the skies to rain showers covering everywhere.

Sainthood is very similar to thunderstorms... Men and women from all over the world decide to say "yes" to the one and true God. Following their Lord wherever and whenever He calls upon them. And thus, their virtues grow and come together to create an amazing show of sounds and echoes of the *Word of God*, with extraordinary lights, reflecting the eternal Light, Jesus Christ. This phenomenon opens the skies, the eternal ones, for showers of grace! A grace that touches every person who seeks the saint's intercession. In addition, while the sounds and lights of thunder storms vanish in seconds, the lightning and thunder of sainthood remain forever!

Saint Charbel Makhlouf was one of these saints who dared to say "yes". He was a simple man like many others, but, through his silence, he provoked a thousand words. A regular Christian whose faith overcame the difficulties of his times, creating a tremendous light of sainthood, still shining all over the Church since the end of the nineteenth century.

So who then is Charbel Makhlouf? How is it possible that an unknown man from an unknown village called Beqaakafra, in a little country called Lebanon, is able to overcome every cultural barrier with his saintly reputation? Why did he develop such a great inspiration in such a short time? How did he manage to heal literally tens of thousands of men and women over the last century?

These above questions need dozens of books to be answered. Nevertheless, we will try to provide some answers in this biography as we look into his life from his birth in Beqaakafra to his death in Saints Peter and Paul's Hermitage in Annaya, along with his canonization on 9th October 1977 at the Vatican.

## Introduction

    This book is divided into four chapters. The first chapter talks about Saint Charbel's childhood and some of the experiences he had and how they shaped him and led him to embrace a religious life. The second chapter tells the years he spent as a monk. The third chapter focuses on his eremitic life. The fourth chapter concentrates on his death and his canonization.

    I hope that, by reading this book, every reader will have enough courage to answer God's call and say yes to His call wherever it leads them on the long and beautiful ways of the Christian life.

# CHAPTER ONE

## FROM BIRTH TO EARLY ADULTHOOD (1828-1851)

*«**My child, conduct your affairs with humility
and you will be loved more than a giver of gifts**.
Humble yourself the more, the greater you are
and you will find favor with God.
The greater you are, the more you must humble
yourself in all things,
and you will find grace before God.
**For great is the power of God;
by the humble he is glorified.**
What is too sublime for you, seek not,
into things beyond your strength search not.
What is committed to you, attend to;
for it is not necessary for you
to see with your eyes
those things which are hidden.
With what is too much for you meddle not,
when shown things beyond human understanding.
Their own opinion has misled many,
and false reasoning unbalanced their judgment.
Where the pupil of the eye is missing,
there is no light, and where there is no
knowledge, there is no wisdom»*

**The Book of Sirach 3:17-24.**

## 1. The Crying of a Newborn

In the early nineteenth century, while Europe and the rest of the world were dealing with the ongoing social, political and economic consequences of the French and industrial revolutions, Mount Lebanon was enjoying rare decades of peace and calm.

As the spring of 1828 was warming the cold icy snow, left from the severe snow storms that hit the Lebanese mountains, the rivers were flowing, and the green grass was filling the sharp edges of the Lebanese cliffs and mountains. The trees blossomed with their wonderful mixture of red, pink, yellow and white flowers and birds came back from their migration destinations to glorify God on those sublime heights. Everything was going forward serenely.

However, the sweet singing of the birds and the sound of water drops from the melting snow was interrupted by the voice of deep innocence… the crying of a newborn on 8th May 1828 in Beqaakafra, a village located in the northern part of the country. The newborn was called Youssef, which means Joseph. He is to become Saint Charbel, who will wipe the tears of the broken souls who ask for his intercession.

Youssef was the fifth child of Antoun and Brigitta Makhlouf who had three boys and two girls: Hanna, Bechara, Kaoneh, Warde and the newborn Youssef[1].

Antoun was a simple peasant who worked hard to be able to provide for his family. His wife Brigitta took care of the children and focused on housework. The Makhlouf's had a small house located on the highest hill in the village. The house was ten meters high and five meters wide. The walls were made very thick to keep the warmth in during winter. The roof was made from wood and soil, just like any other traditional Lebanese house. The inhabitants of the house had to take care of the roof during winter. Every time it snowed, someone had to shovel the snow off the rooftop so the house would not collapse. During summer, lovely evenings were spent

---

[1] H. ISKANDAR, *Saint Charbel From His Contemporaries To Our Era*, Hawk Network Corporation, Lebanon-Antelias 2013, p. 7.

underneath the vineyard planted right at the front door[2].

The region's holy places could be seen from the windows of the house: the Cedars of God pictured in the Old Testament as symbol of glory and pride, the Qadisha Valley the refuge of the Maronite Church in times of persecution, Qadisha eremetic cells, the churches of the near villages and many other places of extraordinary holiness. Beqaakafra itself is considered as holy as the surroundings, it has a church located on each of its borders: the monastery school of Saint Hawchab on its eastern side, Saint Mora's sanctuary on its western side, Saint Saba's church on its southern side and up north the Virgin Mary's parish church[3].

The words spoken at the birth of John the Baptist can also be applied to Youssef: «you, child, will be called prophet of the Most High, for you will go before the Lord to prepare his ways, to give his people knowledge of salvation through the forgiveness of their sins, because of the tender mercy of our God by which the daybreak from on high will visit us to shine on those who sit in

---

[2] G. ABOU SAMRA, *Charbel Ibn Hal Jabal*, Saint Charbel's House, Lebanon-Bekaakafra 2012, p. 5.
[3] G. ABOU SAMRA, *Charbel Ibn Hal Jabal*, Saint Charbel's House, Lebanon-Bekaakafra 2012, p. 7.

darkness and death's shadow, to guide our feet into the path of peace» (Luke 1: 76-79).

## 2. Beqaakafra

Beqaakafra is the highest village in all the Middle East. It is a typical Lebanese village, built at 1650 meters above sea level (5410 ft.). In the early nineteenth century, the humble peasants lived in the villages spread all over Mount Lebanon, by riversides, in the huge valleys and on the top of the hills. The climate forced people living in the northern part of Lebanon, such as Beqaakafra, to work hard in order to overcome snow, fog, rain, steep cliffs and hills. They did their best to work the land and to make a living.

Beqaakafra is surrounded by the highest Lebanese mountains from its southern and eastern sides as it overlooks the Qadisha valley (Qannoubine) the famous Holy Valley. Looking from Beqaakafra to the opposite side of the valley, the village of Bsharri can be seen. Moreover, the oldest Maronite schools in the world are located in that area: Saint George's school of Berqasha built in 1112, Saint Tadros' school of Bsharri built in the 13th century and Our Lady of Hawqa's school, who used to send its students to Rome and Paris, founded in 1624 by the Patriarch Hanna Makhlouf[4].

The Qadisha valley was the best shelter the Maronites had during the long centuries of persecution starting from the fourth century. The valley turned into a holy place throughout the centuries and was filled with hermits and monks. Maronite Patriarchs sought refuge there and lived in Qadisha's monastery for four consecutive centuries in order to escape the savage politics of the Ottoman Emperors. The Ottoman Empire had occupied all the Middle East, including Mount Lebanon, since 1516. The Lebanese population had no choice except submitting itself to the new ruler.

In the Qadisha valley, hundreds of eremitic cells were built meters above the river crossing. These cells were for the many holy people who consecrated their lives to God, and for this reason the valley was known as the Qadisha valley. Qadisha is Syriac for "holy". The river of the Valley emerges under the mountain cliffs where the Cedars of Lebanon, the «Cedars of God», grew next to pine, oak and fir trees.

---

[4] *Op. cit.,* p. 6.

## 3. *His Father Leaves*

In that natural and spiritual surrounding of Bekaakafra, Antoun Makhlouf's family was living its daily life. The core of this family was its Christian faith. Youssef, to become Saint Charbel, was baptized in the Virgin Mary's parish church where villagers gathered every day to participate in the Holy Mass.

Antoun, Youssef's father, was a brave man full of hope and pride. Brigitta, Youssef's mother, used to leave everything and attend the Holy Mass everyday as soon as she heard the bell of the church ringing. Brigitta also persisted in fasting, making it the main instrument of her spirituality. However, her spiritual guide asked her to quit fasting during normal days and to pray the Rosary instead[5]. Hanna, Youssef's brother, was also a vital member to the Christian community. He decided to restore the village's church of Saint Saba while, Warde, Youssef's sister, was never ashamed of praying the Rosary on her way to the village's well or to the fields. Warde's friends once made fun of her saying: «You are holding your prayer beads with you like a nun but you are engaged and when you will get married, your mother in law will never let you pray the Holy

---

[5] P.DAHER, *Saint Charbel*, Saint Maroun's Monastery, Lebanon-Annaya 2012[3], p. 46.

Rosary again». Unfortunately, Warde died even before having the chance to get married[6].

In Beqaakafra's old, narrow and rocky streets, Youssef spent his first three years in peace until one summer night in 1831, when the Makhlouf's family was having dinner and there was a violent knock at the door. Antoun rose up, took a lamp and opened the door. Several soldiers from the Emir Bashir Shehab's army were at the door[7]. Their commander said: «Antoun Makhlouf, starting tomorrow morning you are called to imposed hard labor. You should bring your donkey and come with us to carry provisions for the troops from the village of Mejdlaya to Beiteddine». Antoun objected the order and said: «Officer, I have a family… we are poor peasants… to whom shall I leave my little children?». The officer responded: «This is not our business». Antoun replied: «Give me at least a couple of days so I can find someone to take care of my family». Then, the officer violently shouted: «This is an order! Tomorrow morning… otherwise…».

---

[6] S. GAROFALO, *Il Profumo del Libano*, Postulazione Generale dell'Ordine Libanese Maronita, Italia-Roma 2013[4], p. 65.
[7] H. ISKANDAR, *Saint Charbel From His Contemporaries To Our Era*, Hawk Network Corporation, Lebanon-Antelias 2013, p. 7.

In the morning, Antoun bid his family goodbye and asked his brother Tannous to take care of his beloved ones until he returns. The political situation of the country was very critical. Ibrahim Basha, a General officer in the Egyptian army, had launched campaigns against the Ottoman Empire conquering the Lebanese coast and parts of Syria. This is why the Lebanese Emir Bashir Shehab decided to fight with Ibrahim Basha against the Ottomans, in an attempt to lessen the sorrows of the Lebanese people, since Ibrahim Pasha believed in egalitarianism and he could offer a great possibility of commerce for Mount Lebanon.

## *4. His Father's Death*

On his way back to Beqaakafra, Antoun Makhlouf came down with a severe fever and died at Ghorfeen, nearby Byblos on 8th August 1831[8]. His very poor family was not even able to afford the cost of bringing his corpse back to his native village, so he was buried there. The whole village mourned him on the following day.

---

[8] B. SFEIR, *Ruhaniat Al Keddis Charbel. Chahadat. Taamoulat. Omsulat. Al Jezee Al Awwal. Hadasatahou. Tarahoubahou. Kahanoutahou,* Saint Anthony's Monastery, Lebanon-Ghazir 1995, p.27.

Youssef, his son, was only three years old, and was overwhelmed by great sadness.

Youssef's mother Brigitta was now alone and had to take care of her five children. Tannous, Antoun's brother, continued to help the family until Brigitta got married to Ibrahim Lahud a couple of years after her husband's death. Her new husband was a very good man from the same village.

Maronites, like the other Eastern Catholic and Orthodox Churches, had maintained a long tradition allowing married men to become priests and serve parish churches[9]. So Ibrahim got married to Brigitta and then became a priest. Ibrahim became in charge of a parish near Baalbek, a city in the Bekaa valley. Brigitta's five children stayed at their uncle's house Tannous where he took good care of them and looked after each other. Their mother very often visited them.

Youssef witnessed several other miseries during his early childhood. After his father's death, his uncle's wife, who was a second mother to him died in 1839. Youssef was only eleven years old. In addition, the people revolted against the Egyptian forces and two of Beqaakafra's

---

[9] S. GAROFALO, *Il Profumo del Libano*, Postulazione Generale dell'Ordine Libanese Maronita, Italia-Roma 2013[4], p. 68.

citizens were massacred in 1840. At the age of fourteen, there was an outbreak of cholera in Mount Lebanon, causing great fear, and ended up killing many people including a man from his village[10].

During his early childhood, Youssef learned how to read and write in Saint Hawchab's monastery school. The school teacher was also the village's priest. Therefore, Youssef grew in intelligence, knowledge and faith. He learned several spiritual basics, like going to the Holy Mass and praying the psalms. Youssef loved to play with other children around the village. When he got older, he started working in his family's lands. He dedicated much of his time to keep the land in good condition, since its harvest was the family's main source of income.

## 5. *The Grotto*

Despite the miseries, the inhabitants of Bekaakafra were continuously deepening their faith. Everything surrounding the village created a great combination for inner peace and meditation. In these gorgeous sites, Youssef led his little flock

---

[10] H. ISKANDAR, *Al Keddis Charbel Mn Mouasirih Ila Asrina*, Our Lady of Al Qalaa, Lebanon-Menjez 2009, p. 9.

of sheep to rivers and grassy meadows, allowing them to pasture there.

Youssef used to spend a lot of time pasturing his sheep, away from his family and neighbors. He also spent most of his time in a little grotto down the cliff on the eastern side of the village. It was a silent and serene place where he could pray for long hours without being disturbed. Very often, he would take his cow to the fields, and pray in the grotto while it was pasturing outside. His prayers were very simple and ordinary. If the cow finished pasturing before he was done praying, he would make it wait for him to finish. In the grotto, he had an image of the Virgin Mary in front of which he burned incense and lighted candles.

His friends made fun of him for his constant devotion. However, he was convinced with what he was doing and never stopped praying at that grotto[11]. His friends were gathered one day enjoying themselves and talking, when his cousin Mariam said: «Where is my cousin? Where is Youssef? He stayed with us for a few moments and then disappeared...». The other boys replied: «We don't know where he is. No one knows where he goes... But he is surely praying

---

[11] H. ISKANDAR, *Saint Charbel From His Contemporaries To Our Era*, Hawk Network Corporation, Lebanon-Antelias 2013, p. 8.

somewhere, probably in that grotto where he spends most of his time...»[12].

When Youssef grew older, he started thinking of dedicating himself to Christ through the monastic life. He had started to experience an inner desire of perseverance and faith. When he decided to embrace the monastic life, he prayed a lot to his beloved Virgin Mary, but he was still in need of some advice from his uncles.

## 6. *The Lebanese Maronite Order*

Since the fourth century A.D., the Egyptian desert was populated by ascetics as Saint Athanasius assures[13]. It was initially inhabited by Saint Anthony the Great who shaped Christian monasticism ever since. However, Saint Anthony the Great was not the initiator of Christian monasticism. Several Christian eremitic phenomena had already started to flourish in different regions of the ancient world during the first Christian centuries[14]. The Eastern churches witnessed also Saint Maroun, a contemporary of

---

[12] P. DAHER, *Saint Charbel*, Saint Maroun's Monastery, Lebanon-Annaya 2012³, p. 55.
[13] *Op. cit.*, p. 70.
[14] M. HAYEK, *Tarik Al Sahraa. Al Abb Charbel, Rahib Min Al Charek: 1828-1898*, Editions Xavier Mappus, France-Le Puy 2013, p. 76.

Saint Anthony the Great, the father of the Maronite Church and Maronite monks.

At the beginning of the fourth century and upon Saint Maroun's death, Maroun's followers founded a famous community on the banks of Orontes River with a Monastery dedicated to Saint Maroun as its center. Ever since, the followers were known as the Maronites. Antichalcedonic groups persecuted the Maronites after the Ecumenical Council of Chalcedon of 451 A.D. Unfortunately, three hundred and fifty Maronite monks were killed for accepting that Council[15]. The survivors sent a message to Pope Hormisdas (523 A.D.) explaining their risky situation. These survivors and followers of Saint Maroun were fully recognized by Catholics and Orthodox churches.

Afterwards the Maronites decided to leave the highly dangerous region of Northern Syria and took shelter in the Lebanese mountains. In the Lebanese mountains, they settled, expanded and lived. Through time, a Patriarchal See was founded protecting the community from the savage persecutions they had undergone for centuries. Following this, the Maronites had never stopped their relations with the (Roman Catholic) Apostolic See in Rome, while maintaining their

---

[15] P.DAHER, *Saint Charbel*, Saint Maroun's Monastery, Lebanon-Annaya 2012³, p. 71.

own particular Oriental theological and spiritual tradition.

Several centuries later, on the 10$^{th}$ of November 1695, three young Maronites from Aleppo decided to regroup under the authority of one Superior the monastic communities living in that region. They received the monastic habit from the Patriarch Estephan El-Dowaihy in the Lady of Qannoubeen's monastery in northern Lebanon.

The monks started expanding from the villages of Ehden and Becharri throughout all of Lebanon. They founded the monasteries of Saint John Richmaya in Shoof in 1706, Lady of Louaizi in Keserwan in 1706, Saint Antonious Syr near Rishmaya in 1707, Saint Antonious Kozhaya in 1708 and many other monasteries throughout Lebanon. In 1732, the Pope Clement XII made the monastic rule of these monks official in the Bull «*Apostolatus Officii*». The Order of the monks was called the Lebanese Maronite Order. In 1737, the Order also began expanding outside Lebanon to Cyprus, Rome and Akka.

It is stated in the Constitution of the Lebanese Maronite Order, that the Order is: «one of the authentic monastic life systems... and it goes according to the monastic tradition in the spirit of the Maronite, Syriac and Antioch Church». In fact, the Maronite monks always had an oral tradition for their monastic life until the Lebanese Maronite Order was founded in the seventeenth century[16].

## 7. *Youssef's Uncles*

Youssef Makhlouf had two uncles from Bsharri, Augustine and Daniel Chidiac, who were monks in the Lebanese Maronite Order living in a monastery dedicated to Saint Anthony the Great in Qozhaya. The monastery was a hermitage which provided the opportunity for many to lead an eremitic life of self-giving and sacrifice. Their life, especially the eremitic part of it, had made Youssef very attracted to it. Youssef used to visit his uncles very often to ask for their prayers, guidance and spiritual help.

At Qozhaya's monastery his uncles taught him the history of the Lebanese Maronite Order and the principals of religious and monastic life. «The monk is a person who refuses to live in the joys of this world in order to have the eternal joy of God in return... His only help and treasure is God... By giving everything to God, a monk receives all that could be given in the eternal life...», his uncles used to say.

---

[16] *Op. cit.*, p. 73.

His uncle Father Augustine had also talked to him about the glory of Qozhaya's monastery and about the importance of the Qadisha Valley. He showed him the different places in the Valley and told him the inspiring stories of the oldest Maronite holy places in the world.

The whispers of the praying monks who lived in the valley for centuries could still be heard at the time. The memory of the famous hermit Younan Al-Matriti, who inspired the Maronite Patriarch to be blessed by his holy body before burying him, had not left the valley yet and many other monks who encouraged generations of believers through their writings and testimonies was still continuously glowing in the history of the Maronite Church.

Several monks of that Valley became Bishops and Patriarchs. The first printing machine in the Middle East was also installed in that Valley, in the Qozhaya's Monastery[17]. As Bishop Germanos Farhat said: «Qozhaya is like a moon rising in the horizon of Lebanon and its rays take the penitent by hand and guide him... Its monks are the light of the earth... Armed by angels that protect them,

---

[17] P. DAHER, *Saint Charbel*, Saint Maroun's Monastery, Lebanon-Annaya 2012³, p. 59.

the space of the cells was very tight to contain them»[18].

## 8. *«A Tiny Whispering Sound»*

Every time Youssef visited his uncles or saw the Holy Qadisha Valley, he remembered the fascinating stories and was more and more encouraged to embrace monastic life. He wanted to be like those simple men who received the most precious crown a person can get, the beautiful crown of sainthood.

Youssef had his own life experiences. He faced his father's death. He had seen many hardships in his poor village life. He had also experienced the joy of his brother's and sister's weddings. He had persevered with his daily duties. However, a divine inner voice was saying: «Leave everything and follow Me…»[19].

It was the same quiet whispering heard by Elijah the Prophet long ago that was now being heard by Youssef: «"Go outside and stand on the mountain before the Lord; the Lord will be passing by". Then, a strong and heavy wind was

---

[18] S. GAROFALO, *Il Profumo del Libano*, Postulazione Generale dell'Ordine Libanese Maronita, Italia-Roma 2013[4], p. 74.
[19] P.DAHER, *Saint Charbel*, Saint Maroun's Monastery, Lebanon-Annaya 2012[3], p. 60.

rending the mountains and crushing rocks before the Lord - but the Lord was not in the wind. After the wind there was an earthquake - but the Lord was not in the earthquake. After the earthquake there was fire - but the Lord was not in the fire. After the fire there was a tiny whispering sound, and the Lord was in that sound» (1 Kings 19: 11-12). God, in this tiny whisper, called Youssef to the monastic life, and Youssef in turn was free to accept or turn down this divine call.

## 9. «*Lord, to Whom Whall We Go?*»

At the age of 23, Youssef was ready! He had discovered through the many visits he made to his uncle the nothingness of the mundane earthly life as opposed to the glory of the eternal life. Still, it was difficult to make the decision.

On July 1851, Father Daniel, Youssef's uncle, visited Beqaakafra. When he was leaving, he decided to visit his brother in the monastery of Saint Anthony in Qozhaya and asked Hanna, Youssef's brother if the latter could accompany him. Hanna replied: «I'm afraid that Youssef would go with you and become a monk there in that monastery». Father Daniel answered: «I hope he does, there is nothing more important in this world!».

Eight days later, Youssef left Beqaakafra at dawn heading towards Mayfouq, to the monastery of Our Lady of Mayfouq where his uncle Father Daniel Chidiac lived. He had decided to join the Lebanese Maronite Order in the community of Mayfouq. On that day, Youssef made an ordinary yet a very extraordinary decision. Saying "yes" to God's will is going to change Youssef forever!

Centuries before the birth of Youssef Makhlouf, Jesus' teachings and words scandalized many of his disciples so they decided to leave! So Jesus said to the twelve chosen ones: «What about you, do you want to go away too?» His disciple Peter answered: «Lord, to whom shall we go? You have the words of eternal life» (John 6: 67-68). Eighteenth centuries later, Youssef answered the same answer. To whom shall Youssef go since Christ has the words of eternal life and the brightness of eternal lights?

# CHAPTER TWO

## THE GLORIOUS THUNDER OF A MONK
## (1851-1875)

«*Then shall the just one with great assurance
confront his oppressors
who set at nought his labors.
Seeing this, they shall be shaken
with dreadful fear,
and amazed at the unlooked-for salvation.
They shall say among themselves,
rueful and groaning through anguish of spirit:
"This is he whom once
we held as a laughingstock
and as a type for mockery, fools that we were!
His life we accounted madness,
and his death dishonored.
See how he is accounted among the sons of God;
how his lot is with the saints!
[...] What did our pride avail us?
What have wealth and its boastfulness
afforded us?
All of them passed like a shadow and like a
fleeting rumor;
Like a ship traversing the heaving water,
of which, when it has passed,
no trace can be found*,
*no path of its keel in the waves.
Or like a bird flying through the air;
no evidence of its course is to be found
- But the fluid air,
lashed by the beat of pinions, and cleft by the
rushing force of speeding wings,*

*is traversed: and afterward no mark of passage
can be found in it.
Or as, when an arrow has been shot at a mark,
the parted air straightway flows together again
so that none discerns the way it went through
- Even so we, once born, abruptly came to nought
and held no sign of virtue to display,
but were consumed in our wickedness."
[...]* **But the just live forever,
and in the LORD is their recompense,
and the thought of them is with the Most High.***»*

**The Book of Wisdom 5: 1-5, 8-13, 15.**

## 1. The First Year of the Novitiate

After walking for an entire summer's day, Youssef arrived at the monastery of Our Lady of Mayfouq. He was required to spend two years in that convent for his novitiate. Mayfouq was a simple village but had a long glorious history. It had been the See of the Maronite Patriarchate for two centuries, from the 12$^{th}$ till the 15$^{th}$ century, before the Patriarchs decided to move to Qadisha Valley, escaping the Mamluk Sultanate's persecution. Mayfouq also had a church built on the ruins of an old pagan temple dedicated to the Sun God.

Upon arrival, Youssef knocked on the wooden door of the monastery. He was welcomed by the monks and told them he had come all the way from Beqaakafra to join the order. He was immediately received by the Superior of the convent. At the time, when young men joined monasteries, they did not need special recommendations from anyone, they only had to introduce themselves, where they came from, and why they are joining the monastic life[1]. On the evening of that summer day, the Father Superior asked him in front of the other monks: «What are you seeking in this place?». Youssef answered him: «I am looking for the glory of God and the salvation of my soul»[2].

For eight days, Youssef remained in his secular clothes as was the norm. The procedure was practiced in order to give time to examine the person's willingness to take up that kind of life. At the end of the eighth day, Youssef received a new black habit and a black belt; it was the habit of the Lebanese Maronite monks.

Youssef had the freedom to choose between changing his name or not, but he decided to change it to Charbel. Charbel was a holy martyr, the bishop of Edessa, who lived during the first two centuries A.D. Charbel of Edessa was also Saint Barbara's brother and he was killed during the persecutions led by the Emperor

---

[1] M. HAYEK, *Tarik Al Sahraa. Al Abb Charbel, Rahib Min Al Charek: 1828-1898*, Editions Xavier Mappus, France-Le Puy 2013, p. 72.
[2] P. DAHER, *Saint Charbel*, Saint Maroun's Monastery, Lebanon-Annaya 2012³, p. 74.

Trajan at the beginning of the second century[3]. The commemoration of this Saint of Edessa is on the 5th of September in the Maronite Church[4]. There are ruins of a Church dedicated to the martyr of Edessa, near Bsharri, close to Youssef's native village, which might explain why he decided to take the name Charbel.

With this new beginning, Youssef left everything behind: his parents, his lifestyle and his village. He was not Youssef anymore; from now on he was to be known as Charbel, a man preparing himself to spend the rest of his life with his Savior. A life lived with Jesus Christ, a life that is going to be known decades later throughout the world...

## 2. «*Is Fit for the Kingdom of God*»

After leaving his native village, Youssef's family was worried for him. They started looking for him. He did not inform anyone about his departure. No one in Bekaakafra knew that Youssef's intention was to start his novitiate in Mayfouq. When the family heard of his choice,

---

[3] S. GAROFALO, *Il Profumo del Libano*, Postulazione Generale dell'Ordine Libanese Maronita, Italia-Roma 2013[4], p. 80.

[4] Saint Charbel of Edessa is commemorated on the 29th of January in the Roman Catholic Church.

they were not convinced that it was his vocation. His uncle refused the idea of him becoming Brother Charbel. His uncle was a very poor peasant and Youssef was necessary help for him. His family could not just let go of him. Everyone had his or her own reasons to stop Youssef from pursing religious life.

His uncle and guardian Tannous, who took care of the family upon the death of his father, went to Mayfouq to bring Youssef back home. Tannous was followed by Youssef's mother and brothers who helplessly tried to bring him back home to Bekaakafra[5]. All their attempts failed... They were not taking into consideration the divine plan for Youssef. His family did not know the profound and peaceful spiritual encounter that Charbel was having with the Lord.

The family tried to bring him back several other times in 1851. His mother once went to Mayfouq with his uncle Tannous and waited outside the monastery until the novitiates went out to work the land. The novitiates came out one by one and when she spotted her son, Brigitta immediately ran after him and grabbed his black religious habit and said: «Come home with

---

[5] B. SFEIR, *Ruhaniat Al Keddis Charbel. Chahadat. Taamoulat. Omsulat. Al Jezee Al Awwal. Hadasatahou. Tarahoubahou. Kahanoutahou*, Saint Anthony's Monastery, Lebanon-Ghazir 1995, p. 106.

me...». But Charbel went on and followed his brothers[6].

Charbel's determination to follow his Lord Jesus and dedicate his life to Him, challenged the whole family. His mother was in deep sorrow[7] and was truly disappointed because of her own expectations... she had not known that God was preparing great glory for her son; a glory that will never pass, an eternal life of joy and greatness. How could she know what Jesus Christ was preparing for her son? She was only trying to do what she thought was the best for Charbel!

By turning down all these attempts, Charbel became more determined in his desire for monastic life. As the Lord Jesus said: «Once the hand is laid on the plough, no one who looks back is fit for the kingdom of God» (Luke 9: 62), this is what Charbel was doing: once he entered religious life, he did not look backwards again.

## 3. *The Novitiate's Life*

Charbel studied the Rule of the novitiate in the first eight days he spent in the monastery

---

[6] H. ISKANDAR, *Saint Charbel From His Contemporaries To Our Era*, Hawk Network Corporation, Lebanon-Antelias 2013, p. 9.
[7] *Ibidem.*

before receiving the habit. He knew now that the novice must imitate the Lord Jesus Christ, obey with joy and happiness and respect his Superior as he respects Christ himself. In addition, he must know that the purpose of obedience is to sacrifice his personal will so he can be totally in tune with the will of God, as expressed by his Superior. Every testimony given after Charbel's death confirmed that Charbel's observance of the novitiate rule was sacred and his obedience was angelic; none of the testimonies mentioned that he rebelled against his Superiors.

During the first year of novitiate, young Charbel lived a life of prayer, work, education and religious formation. The novitiate is an intensive year that tries to develop the person's spiritual life, so he could discern whether he is willing to live this life and adopt an ascetical lifestyle. Liturgy and personal prayers are the most important tasks of the future monk[8] and this is why the Liturgy of the hours (Divine Office) was obligatory to help the novices communicate with God. The novices were also scheduled to wake up for midnight prayer and meditation. Every day from dawn, they started their day with prayers. During the week, they were supposed to

---

[8] S. GAROFALO, *Il Profumo del Libano*, Postulazione Generale dell'Ordine Libanese Maronita, Italia-Roma 2013[4], p. 83.

keep liturgical traditions alive and learn the beautiful Antiochian Maronite liturgical hymns.

In order to better understand the spirituality of the Order, novices also used to study the Rule and Constitutions of the Order and learned about Order's history. They also used to deepen their knowledge regarding the Christian faith and learn about the sacraments/mysteries of the Church. It was very important for a monk to know how to confess his sins, participate in the Divine Liturgy (Mass) and live his religious life as it should be lived.

The novitiate was a time of grace and also of challenges. It was a time of discernment. The novice had to learn how to make bread, wash clothes, prepare wood for winter, do carpentry work, make shoes, work the land...[9] Not all the novices would manage to finish the novitiate. Nevertheless, Charbel was going forward as days went on, without any complaints. The Holy Spirit, who led him to Mayfouq, was constantly with him.

---

[9] P. DAHER, *Saint Charbel*, Saint Maroun's Monastery, Lebanon-Annaya 2012$^3$, p. 80.

## *4. Annaya*

During the novitiate, novices used to silk farm, an agriculture very famous in Mount Lebanon at that time. For this reason, novices used to collect the mulberries, while women and girls fed the silkworms[10]. While they were collecting mulberries, a girl noticed the strict behavior of Brother Charbel and decided to throw a silkworm on him while she was standing on the ladder, then she went down and put the silkworm on his hand, in order to distract him.

On that day, Charbel came to the conclusion that he could no longer stay at the monastery of Mayfouq. This was based on two reasons: first, the persistent visits of his parents became troubling for Charbel because they were effecting that glowing peaceful light of faith and hope inside his heart. Second, it made no sense for him to let any kind of temptation interfere his religious vocation, so he made the decision to go to Saint Maroun's monastery in Annaya. The village was a two-hour walk from Mayfouq and its monastery was particularly distant from lay people.

---

[10] H. ISKANDAR, *Saint Charbel From His Contemporaries To Our Era*, Hawk Network Corporation, Lebanon-Antelias 2013, p. 9.

In the archive of the monastery of Mayfouq, the monks wrote in Arabic that Charbel had freely left the ecclesiastical status without any pressure[11]. His brother Hanna living in Beqaakafra, was extremely distressed to hear that his brother left the monastery voluntarily but was relieved when he knew that he headed to the monastery of Annaya.

On his way to Annaya, Charbel had the chance to pass by Lehfed and Mishmish, two old Maronite villages. From a distance, he could oversee Annaya's monastery lying on a beautiful hill of green trees. When he arrived to Annaya, Charbel explained his intentions to the Superior, who accepted him after asking the permission of the Superior General.

### 5. *The End of the Novitiate*

Annaya's monastery of Saint Maroun is located on a hill. In 1798, thirty years before Charbel's birth, the Lebanese Maronite Order initially constructed a hermitage on that hill. Thirty years later in 1828, the monks bought a land and founded the monastery of Saint Maroun near the hermitage.

---

[11] H. ISKANDAR, *Saint Charbel From His Contemporaries To Our Era*, Hawk Network Corporation, Lebanon-Antelias 2013, p. 9.

In that monastery, Charbel continued his journey in the novitiate. His second year was very similar to the first. He learned to spend more time and dedicate more effort to fight temptations and to offer hidden sacrifices. Working in the fields, the novices and monks had to remain silent and meditate in the presence of God. They also had to surrender to the requests of their Superiors. In fact, they were not allowed to say a word in front of their Superiors and only respond if they were addressed. In the dining room, the novices sat far from the Superior but when he passed in front of them, they had to rise, bow and look at the ground having their hands crossed above their chests. If any novice deserved a rebuke, he had to kneel at once and listen to it silently[12].

At the end of October 1853, it was time for the monks to prepare for the beautiful ceremony of solemn vows. During this era, it was possible to make solemn vows directly. The ceremony was preceded by a personal encounter of the monastery's monks with the novice-master during which he asked whether the novices were to be accepted in the Order or not. The encounters were followed by a ritual, consisting of passing around a cap and asking each monk to drop a grain of

---

[12] S. GAROFALO, *Il Profumo del Libano*, Postulazione Generale dell'Ordine Libanese Maronita, Italia-Roma 2013[4], p. 83.

wheat for consensus or a grain of barley for disapproval of accepting the novice in the Order.

On the 1st of November 1853, the novitiate period was over. The monks had decided to accept Charbel into their Order, and there he was with his fellow brothers dressed in white, barefoot and waiting to offer himself forever to his Lord and God. When the Holy Mass started, the novices entered the church singing Psalm 50 with the choir: «Have mercy on me, O God...»[13]. During the Holy Mass, Charbel went to the altar, kneeled and took the solemn lifetime vows of obedience, chastity and poverty.

Charbel gave himself to his Lord without reservation. He decided to say an eternal "yes", that he renewed everyday with small acts of faith, hope and charity. From that moment, he became always aware and lived in God's presence, encountering Jesus Christ on a daily basis.

## 6. *In Heaven We Shall meet*

Slightly before his solemn vows, Brigitta, Charbel's mother, decided to visit him at Annaya's monastery. She insisted on seeing him, but he refused to see her. He spoke to her through

---

[13] P. Daher, *Charbel. Insan Sekran Bi Allah*, Saint Maroun's Monastery, Lebanon-Annaya 1978², p. 81.

the window, without letting her see him. She immediately blamed him saying: «How is it… You prohibit me from seeing you?». He responded: «In heaven we shall meet…». Her efforts were to no avail, so Brigitta reluctantly returned to her village[14].

On that day, Brother Charbel did not intend to hurt his mother's feelings. He was only trying to remain faithful to the novitiate's rule which forbids meeting any person except for the monastery's monks. His mother could not understand this.

What his mother could not understand is actually written in the first chapter of the book of Jeremiah from the Old Testament. It is written in that book that the word of God came to a young man, Jeremiah, and said: «Before I formed you in the womb I knew you; before you came to birth I consecrated you; I appointed you as prophet to the nations». Then Jeremiah said, «Ah, ah, ah, Lord; you see, I do not know how to speak: I am too young!». But the Lord replied, «Say not, "I am too young". To whomever I send you, you shall go; whatever I command you, you shall speak. Have no fear before them, because I am with you to deliver you, says the Lord» (Jeremiah 1: 5-8).

---

[14] H. Iskandar, *Saint Charbel From His Contemporaries To Our Era*, Hawk Network Corporation, Lebanon-Antelias 2013, p. 9.

God had chosen Charbel years before he moved to Mayfouq. God saw the Saint Charbel even before his mother had the chance to know Charbel and give him birth. Charbel's choice was not against his parents, it was a profound "yes" to the eternal love of God.

## 7. *Kfifan*

In 1853, slightly after the solemn vows of the brothers, the Superior of Saint Maroun's monastery called Brother Charbel and told him: «Son, your novitiate is over. The General Superior has assigned you to move to Saint Cyprian and Justina's monastery of Kfifan so you can dedicate yourself to the necessary priesthood studies. Tomorrow morning you shall behead there»[15]. Therefore, the obedient man of God went the next day to Kfifan, crossing the village of Mayfouq where he had spent his first year of novitiate. On his arrival to Kfifan, the fifty monks residing in that monastery welcomed him with great joy. He met with Father Nimatullah El-Kafri, an intelligent monk, who was the principal of the school and also taught there.

At that school, the Lebanese Maronite brothers of Kfifan were assigned another teacher,

---

[15] P. DAHER, *Saint Charbel*, Saint Maroun's Monastery, Lebanon-Annaya 2012³, p. 91.

Father Nimatullah Kassab, who was Father Nimatullah El-Kafri's deputy. Students used to study philosophy and theology in that monastery. Philosophy was necessary to the understand theology and theological studies were crucial for the priesthood preparation. The courses consisted of studying the Holy Scriptures, Moral issues and difficulties that a priest could encounter during confession or when consulted. In addition to that, special theological courses aimed at to explain heretic and false doctrines[16]. The studies also covered Arabic, the spoken language of the country and Syriac, the language of the Maronite Liturgy. The great Syriac Church Fathers such as Saint Ephrem and Jacob of Serugh were continuously read in the prayers adopted in the books of prayers. Their hymns and prayers were the heart of the Maronite Liturgy lived in that monastery[17].

During their time at the school of Kfifan, the brothers were also invited to practice everything they learned about the religious life during their novitiate and deepen their knowledge of Christian and monastic virtues. Charbel was well known by his fellow brothers and Superiors

---

[16] S. GAROFALO, *Il Profumo del Libano*, Postulazione Generale dell'Ordine Libanese Maronita, Italia-Roma 2013[4], p. 96.
[17] *Op. cit.*, p. 97.

as an excellent student. However, the greatest lessons Charbel learned at Kfifan were given to him from his relationship to the Lord Jesus. He learned to listen to the tender voice of the Lord deep inside his heart. He kneeled for long hours in the church praying and talking with his Savior.

## 8. *Father Nimatullah Kassab*

In Kfifan, Charbel also met the 45-year-old Father Nimatullah Kassab, an Assistant General in the Lebanese Maronite Order at the time. Father Kassab was famous for his profound faith and holiness. When Father El-Kafri could not teach in the school of Kfifan, Father Nimatullah Kassab replaced him.

Father Nimatullah Kassab was born in the village of Hardine in 1808. He joined the Lebanese Maronite Order and made his solemn vows in 1830 after the novitiate period. He was ordained a priest on 25th December 1833[18]. Nimatullah was known to be a man of great virtues. It is said in biographies written about him that he used to confess his sins daily in preparation for Holy Mass and then offered Holy Mass with great devotion and prayer. Likewise, Nimatullah never ate his lunch before praying the

---

[18] http://www.vatican.va/news_services/liturgy/saints/ns_lit_doc_20040516_al-hardini_en.html

whole Rosary. He fasted daily for 25 years, starting the day of his priesthood ordination until his death.

Father Nimatullah Kassab accepted the role of Assistant General for three times, only after he was asked to accept it out of obedience[19]. Poverty infiltrated every aspect of his life from food to clothing and his austere sleeping condition. His humility was clearly noticed. When anyone told him he was a well-mannered monk and deserved to be the Superior General of the Order, Nimatullah responded: «I would rather die».

Father Nimatullah prayed constantly. His heart burned with love for the Blessed Sacrament and for the Virgin Mary[20]. He spent his days in prayer, meditation, fasting and work. He used to pray during the night instead of sleeping[21], without letting that affect his perseverance to work hard during the daytime. On his canonical visits to the monasteries of the Order, he and the General Superior preferred to sleep on the ground

---

[19] S. GAROFALO, *Il Profumo del Libano*, Postulazione Generale dell'Ordine Libanese Maronita, Italia-Roma 2013⁴, p. 103.
[20] M. HAYEK, *Tarik Al Sahraa. Al Abb Charbel, Rahib Min Al Charek: 1828-1898*, Editions Xavier Mappus, France-Le Puy 2013, p. 92.
[21] Y. KHACHAN, *Al Kawakib Al Khamsa*, Lebanese Maronite Order, 1996³, p. 125.

instead of sleeping on beds. Father Nimatullah Kassab and the General Superior also used to wake up very often before midnight prayer and wash the dishes prior to waking the other monks for the morning prayer.

On 14th December 1858, Father Nimatullah Kassab passed away. In the last moments of his life, he was holding an icon of the Blessed Virgin and saying: «O Mary, to you I entrust my soul». Father Nimatullah Kassab was canonized by Pope John Paul II, at the Vatican on 16th May 2004. Saint Nimatullah Kassab was a huge inspiration for the young Charbel Makhlouf. Nimatullah said once about Charbel: «I have a student who is a saint, his name is Brother Charbel from Bekaakafra».

## 9. «*Do This in Remembrance of Me*»

At the Last Supper, when Jesus was with his disciples, he «took the bread, said the blessing, broke it, and gave it to them, saying: "This is my body, which will be given for you; do this in memory of me". And likewise the cup after they had eaten, saying: "This cup is the new covenant in my blood, which will be shed for you"» (Luke 22: 19-20).

On 23rd July 1859, the day came for Charbel to celebrate Holy Mass in remembrance of Christ, as a newly ordained priest, at the age of thirty one. His yearning and desire to offer himself to Jesus was fully realized. On that day of July, Bishop Youssef El-Marid, delegated by Patriarch Paul Massaad, laid his hands on Charbel's head in Bkerke. There, God had sworn an oath he will never retract; Charbel is now a priest forever in the order of Melchizedek (Psalm 110: 4).

Following the Maronite Liturgy of Priesthood Ordination, Charbel was vested in the liturgical clothes of priesthood. Then he was asked to make three rounds inside the church as written by the Liturgy. During the first round, he incenses the people of God. On the second, he is given the book of the Holy Gospel as he will proclaim it to the whole Church. On the last round, he takes the chalice containing the consecrated bread and wine, puts it on his head and goes around for the last time, as a servant of the body of Christ.

From that day on, all Charbel's life will become in remembrance of Jesus Christ. He daily celebrated the Holy Mass. His life, acts, words, silence, prayers and meditations all aimed to glorify the Lord. The little inner glowing light conveyed on the day of his baptism, which had further glowed during his novitiate, was day by day becoming a magnificent source of peace for the son of Bekaakafra.

After his Ordination, Charbel was asked to return to Annaya's Saint Maroun monastery where he had spent his second year of novitiate. Upon his arrival, he found his relatives waiting for him[22]. His mother could not make it to participate to his ordination in Bkerke since she was too old to take the journey. His family asked him if he could go to his native village Bekaakafra to celebrate his first Mass, but he refused, citing the monastic rule: «the monk who turns back to his village after taking his vows, should repeat the novitiate»[23].

---

[22] P. DAHER, *Saint Charbel*, Saint Maroun's Monastery, Lebanon-Annaya 2012³, p. 97.
[23] H. ISKANDAR, *Saint Charbel From His Contemporaries To Our Era*, Hawk Network Corporation, Lebanon-Antelias 2013, p. 10.

# CHAPTER THREE

## The Eternal Light of a Hermit (1875-1898)

*«Now will I praise those godly men,*
*our ancestors, each in his own time:*
*The abounding glory of the Most High's portion,*
*his own part, since the days of old.*
*Subduers of the land in kingly fashion,*
*men of renown for their might,*
*or counselors in their prudence,*
*or seers of all things in prophecy;*
*Resolute princes of the folk,*
*and governors with their staves;*
*Authors skilled in composition,*
*and forgers of epigrams with their spikes;*
*Composers of melodious psalms,*
*or discoursers on lyric themes;*
*Stalwart men, solidly established*
*and at peace in their own estates*
*-* **All these were glorious in their time,**
**each illustrious in his day**.
*Some of them have left behind a name*
*and men recount their praiseworthy deeds;*
**But of others there is no memory,**
**for when they ceased, they ceased**.
*And they are as though they had not lived,*
*they and their children after them.*
**Yet these also were godly men whose virtues**
**have not been forgotten**;
*their wealth remains in their families,*
*their heritage with their descendants;*
*Through God's covenant with them*
*their family endures,*

*their posterity, for their sake.
And for all time their progeny will endure,
their glory will never be blotted out;*
**Their bodies are peacefully laid away,
but their name lives on and on.**
*At gatherings their wisdom is retold,
and the assembly proclaims their praise»*

**The Book of Sirach 44: 1-15.**

## 1. Sixteen Years

Charbel lived for sixteen years in the spirit of silence at Saint Maroun's monastery in Annaya. The monks' prayers were heard in the foothills of that mountain, and only interrupted by the voice of nature and the ringing bells, announcing prayer time. Charbel never used to wait for the bell in order to commence his prayers. His whole life was a continuous prayer.

Like in other communities, the monks' life in Annaya used to have its tensions and fraternal disagreements. Since the 1832 Council held by the Order, several groups started to form inside the Lebanese Maronite Order. These groups were based on the monks' origins. The inner monastic tensions grew day after day[1] and made the Superior General's life very difficult.

---

[1] H. ISKANDAR, *Al Keddis Charbel Mn Mouasirih Ila Asrina*, Our Lady of Al Qalaa, Lebanon-Menjez 2009, p. 23.

Mount Lebanon was facing much turmoil during those years. In 1840, the Ottomans retreated after the Convention of London took place following the Egyptian war. Their withdrawal incited a civil war between Christians and Muslims in Mount Lebanon which resulted in a great misery. Charbel was only twelve years old at the time. In 1858, while the thirty-year-old Charbel was studying in Kfifan, poor peasants led a revolution against the feudal authorities of Keserwan, generating hatred and murders. By the time Charbel became a priest, another civil war had started in Mount Lebanon in 1860. The Ottomans roused the Druze and Muslims against the Christian villages and targeted the villages in Chouf, Matn and Zahle's regions, killing its people and burning houses and churches[2]. Charbel, with a lot of courage, took the Lord as his shepherd and was not afraid during these events. The Lord's "staff and crook" were always there to comfort him (Psalm 23: 4).

In addition to the clashes, the monastic rule was very tough. It consisted of long hours of work and prayer. Prayers were not only held during the day; the monks also had to wake up at midnight to pray. However, Charbel always looked for the right balance in order to keep focusing on his

---

[2] P. DAHER, *Saint Charbel*, Saint Maroun's Monastery, Lebanon-Annaya 2012³, p. 158.

journey. When he was instructed to go and pray for a suffering or sick person, he would go out of obedience and with much joy. When he was asked to work the land, he used to do it with remarkable dedication. He enjoyed reading the book, *The Imitation of Christ* and prayed the Rosary daily.

Father Charbel wore thin old clothes during the cold Lebanese winters. During the coldest days, when everyone was freezing, he did not wear thicker clothes. He was satisfied with the simple clothes he had[3]. His main focus was on taking care of the land and the surrounding trees. His worked conscientiously in order to purify his heart. On the other hand, he was doing great sacrifices to stay faithful to the vow of obedience, trying to do whatever he was asked, for the glory of God and for the salvation of souls.

Day by day, he got closer to monastic perfection. He stayed for sixteen years in the monastery of Saint Maroun before moving to the nearby hermitage[4]. He embodied what Saint Paul advocated in his letter to the Romans: «I urge you therefore, brothers, by the mercies of God, to

---

[3] A. CHEBLI, *Al Abb Charbel Makhlouf. Mn Abnaa Al Rahbania Al Baladya Al Lubnania Al Marounia. Habis Mahbasit Deir Annaya*, Saint Maroun Monastery, Lebanon-Annaya 1999², p. 18.

[4] P. DAHER, *Saint Charbel*, Saint Maroun's Monastery, Lebanon-Annaya 2012³, p. 97.

offer your bodies as a living sacrifice, holy and pleasing to God, your spiritual worship. Do not conform yourselves to this age but be transformed by the renewal of your mind, that you may discern what is the will of God, what is good and pleasing and perfect. For by the grace given to me I tell everyone among you not to think of himself more highly than one ought to think, but to think soberly, each according to the measure of faith that God has apportioned» (Romans 12: 1-3).

## 2. «*The Hill of Transfiguration*»

The monastic rule, which Saint Charbel had vowed states: «Since our Fathers cultivated not only coenobitic life, but also the eremitic one and handed it down to us; therefore, true to this tradition, it is acceptable for every professed monk, after five years of monastic profession, and after asking and having the permission of the Abbot, to withdraw, temporally or permanently from public life. A separated cell in the monastic community is provided for the exclusive living of the monk according to the judgment of the Abbot and of the Congregation. There, he will dedicate himself to prayer and spiritual exercises. In addition, a small field for cultivation will be entrusted to him, in case he is in good health, or he will attend to a useful and convenient handwork. Then the Abbot, before giving the monk permission, will test his soul, so that withdrawal does not expose him to the deception of the Devil.[5]

According to the above rule, the Maronite monks had the opportunity to establish hermitages. And near the monastery of Saint Maroun, on the hill called "the Hill of Transfiguration", a hermitage dedicated to Saint Peter and Paul was built. It was around 1400 meters (4590 feet) above sea level. The hermitage was a ground floor house divided into two parts by a long corridor that ends up on its eastern side with an arch opened towards the north.

The little church of Saint Peter and Paul's hermitage was located in its southern part, connected to the corridor with a door opening to the west allowing the public to enter and participate in the Holy Mass. The cells of the hermits were situated on the opposite side of the corridor. The roof is two to three meters high (6.5 to 10 foot) and made from wood. A wall surrounding the hermitage was often struck by thunder during winter[6].

---

[5] S. GAROFALO, *Il Profumo del Libano*, Postulazione Generale dell'Ordine Libanese Maronita, Italia-Roma 2013[4], p. 199.
[6] H. ISKANDAR, *Saint Charbel From His Contemporaries To Our Era*, Hawk Network Corporation, Lebanon-Antelias 2013, p. 11.

The first hermit to inhabit that place on 29th November 1829 was Father Alishaa Kassab, Father Nimatullah Kassab's brother. Father Alishaa paved the ground of the hermitage and planted vineyards on the eastern side. He dedicated a lot of effort to expand the property of the hermitage.

## 3. The Miracle of the Lamp

In 1875, the forty-seven-year-old Father Charbel, officially asked to live in holy silence at Annaya's hermitage. It had been twenty-one years since he took his solemn vows and so he had the right to ask permission to move to the hermitage. During that year, Father Alishaa who lived in that hermitage, died on 13th February. When Charbel asked to leave the monastery of Saint Maroun and become a hermit, the Superior did not accept his request; he was probably waiting for a divine sign.

A few days after, the Superior, Father Elias Meshmeshani, rang the bell of the dining room and said: «Starting tonight, no one is to light his oil lamp after dinner, so we can all save oil for midnight prayer. It is an order so be obedient in following the prohibition». On the same night, Charbel returned late from the fields peacefully carrying the agricultural equipment and went straight to his room. He tried to light his oil lamp, but was not able to do so. He noticed the lamp was missing oil. He went to Brother Francis, who was responsible for filling the lamps with oil. On his way, he saw two of the servants washing dishes. He gently asked them if they could fill his lamp with oil, without knowing about the prohibition. Then Father Charbel went to his room and waited for the filled lamp. But one of the servants, a young boy, put a bench in the dark corridor to mess with Father Charbel. The peaceful Father stumbled and fell on the ground but got on his feet immediately and continued to his room without saying a word.

The servant knew about the prohibition of filling the monks' lamps with oil, and so he filled Father Charbel's lamp with water instead of oil and headed to Charbel's room. His fellow servant stopped him and asked him to stop messing with Father Charbel, but he refused to listen. The gentle Father Charbel opened the door of his room, took the lamp from the servant, closed the door and turned the lamp on! It was filled with water, yet it was burning! The cheeky servant was shocked to see the light coming out of Father Charbel's room. So, he immediately ran to his fellow servant and called him. Both of them started to talk about this, trying to understand if Father Charbel had another lamp in his room. If he had another one, then why would he ask to fill the empty one? And if he had not, how could he turn this one on when it was filled with water?

At that point, the Father Superior Elias woke up and heard the servants whispering about the light they saw coming out of Father Charbel's room. Father Elias asked the servants what was going on. The young servant immediately confessed to filling Father Charbel's lamp with water. The Superior stood there with a perplexed expression. How was it possible that Father Charbel, the example of obedience in the monastery, was disobeying?! Consequently, the Superior knocked on Father Charbel's door and asked: «Why is your oil lamp turned on despite the prohibition?». At once, Father Charbel got down on his knees and said: «Forgive me dear Father. I did not know anything about the prohibition you are talking about». Then, Father Elias took Charbel's lamp emptied some of the liquid in his hand and examined it… It was water! As a result, Father Elias knelt in front of Father Charbel, asking him for forgiveness. On the following day, seeing the heavenly sign regarding the substitution of oil with water, Father Elias told the Superior General and the Patriarch about the incident. Hearing about the unusual episode, they gave permission to Father Charbel to join Saint

Peter and Paul's Hermitage which he did on 15th February 1875[7].

## 4. Many Battles He Had Won

On that same evening, Father Charbel was to move to the Hermitage of Annaya; he had already won a thousand spiritual battles and yet a thousand more were to be won. Twenty-four years after leaving his native village Beqaakafra to the novitiate of Mayfouq, Charbel was living his priesthood, filled with patience, wisdom, courage, devotion and dedication.

Similar to gemstones that get their glow and colors under huge pressure and extreme temperatures, Father Charbel's virtues were glowing day after day under the pressure of daily difficulties and extreme temptations. A monk's life is not an easy life. However, every difficulty could become a privileged way of growing further in grace and sainthood because «God works with those who love him, those who have been called in accordance with his purpose and turns everything to their good» (Romans 8: 28).

Father Charbel became well known in the monastery of Saint Maroun for his love of God

---

[7] P. DAHER, *Saint Charbel*, Saint Maroun's Monastery, Lebanon-Annaya 2012[3], p. 122.

with all his heart, his soul and his mind and for loving his neighbor as himself (Matthew 22: 37-39). He also became well known for his faith and hope, his supreme prudence, his extraordinary justice and his ideal conviction and rare courage. Charbel had grown and became strong in spirit, and he was in the «desert» of the hermitage until the day he appeared to the people of God[8].

Like the winter snow of Lebanon which infiltrates the rocks of high mountains and flows out into the great clear spring rivers, the Holy Mass, the liturgical hymns, the Sacred Scriptures and the few Christian classics that Charbel had, such as the *Imitation of Christ*, the *Preparation for Death* by Saint Alphonsus De Liguori[9] and biographies of some saints, have now slowly catalyzed Charbel's spiritual growth. Every grace he received, prayer he held, or Mass he celebrated is by now an immense treasure of serenity, lying into Charbel's heart, waiting the moment of peaceful emanation. When the time will come, all the work God operated with his beloved Charbel will be revealed through eternal light of sainthood.

---

[8] Cf. Luke 1: 80
[9] S. GAROFALO, *Il Profumo del Libano*, Postulazione Generale dell'Ordine Libanese Maronita, Italia-Roma 2013[4], p. 135.

## 5. His Daily Life in the Hermitage

Days serenely passed in the hermitage. Every day Father Charbel woke up in time for morning prayer. He used to take his prayer book, sit in the little chapel and wait the prayer to begin. After morning prayer, he used to grab his shovel and take off for work. He always had his rosary prayer beads with him. Working the vineyard, he did it with great dedication, meditation and very often in silence. When his fellow workers rested and talked, he went away and remained silent. When the bell rang for midday prayer, he kneeled on the soil or on the rocks and prayed. He celebrated Holy Mass at noon. At two o'clock, everyone was called to lunch, so Father Charbel ate in silence. In the afternoon, he worked again until sunset[10]. In the evening, another liturgical prayer was celebrated, and the hermits woke up at midnight to start the first minutes of every day praising God for his wonders. Father Charbel used to confess once a week, persevering in the spiritual battle.

In the hermitage, Charbel experienced many glorious events that reflected his true faith. His brother once arrived from Bekaakafra to visit him, he knocked on the door and waited... Father

---

[10] H. ISKANDAR, *Saint Charbel From His Contemporaries To Our Era*, Hawk Network Corporation, Lebanon-Antelias 2013, p. 15.

Charbel asked: «Who is there?», his brother responded: «I am Father Charbel's brother and I would like to see him». Father Charbel went to Father Makarious and asked him if he is allowed to meet his brother. Father Makarious instantly gave him the permission to do so. Charbel did not want to disobey the eremitic rule even in its slightest details. He saw his brother and asked him about his family in Bekaakafra, especially about their spiritual life.

On another occasion, Father Charbel's niece Warde came to the hermitage, bringing him some "good news". Charbel had inherited a land from his brother and he could claim the right to its possession. The humble hermit, who had gone through a very long journey of poverty, told her: «I no longer have any attachment to this world. My brother died this year, but I died since the day I left my village. Whoever is dead neither inherits nor leaves an inheritance». But Father Charbel will leave this world a beautiful patrimony, a precious inheritance that no human being can imagine, the treasure of his spiritual experience.

## 6. *His Vows and Theological Virtues*

The three vows of religious life consist in a demanding and privileged way to reach heaven. Father Charbel lived the vow of poverty like many of his predecessors. He renounced all kinds of material possessions and accepted God through the Blessed Sacrament as his only way for prosperity and happiness. It is a true and authentic act of faith to accept and admit that Christ himself can be the treasure of one's life. Charbel somehow lived what Saint Ephrem said about the Holy Body and Blood of Christ in his hymn called "Christ and His Church": «In death, husbands are separated from their wives and wives from their husbands. However, in the case of the Church, the glorious spouse, with the death of its Husband (Christ), it was united to Him in a pure and immaculate way. And after Christ's death, the Church took his body daily, broke it, ate it, tasted it, worshiped it and thanked it because he saved the Church from straying»[11]. The Blessed Sacrament became Father Charbel's greatest treasure.

On the other hand, the vow of obedience is a slow martyrdom. It is a total offering of love and charity. No monk can sincerely and peacefully obey if he is not filled with the love of Christ and respect for his Superiors. Adam and

---

[11] B. SFEIR, *Ruhaniat Al Keddis Charbel. Chahadat. Taamoulat. Omsulat. Al Jezee Al Sani. Hayatihi el Dayria. Dikatihi fi Hifzi el Kawanin. Fadailihi el Ilahia wal Adabia*, Saint Anthony's Monastery, Lebanon-Ghazir 1996, p 35.

Eve rebelled against God and his commandment, but Father Charbel obeyed his Superior and by such, obeyed the Lord and His commandments, especially the final one given to His disciples during the Last Supper: «Love one another just as I have loved you» (John 13: 34).

While striving after perfecting two of the vows, it is unwise to leave the third one untouched. It would be like constructing a building only on the two thirds of its foundations and risking the collapse of the building at any moment. Therefore, Father Charbel always tried to persevere in chastity. The biggest achievement Charbel made regarding chastity was not surely avoiding women since it must be easy for a monk or a hermit to do so. His biggest achievement was to recognize that the graces he received were from the Holy Spirit, that sainthood was a gift and that God is his only Lord.

## 7. Prudence and Justice

Prudence knows how to create a good balance between spiritual and physical life. Prudence guides other virtues by setting measures and rules[12]. Father Charbel can be surely identified as a prudent man. Despite all the fasts

---

[12] Catechism of the Catholic Church, number 1806.

and ascetic deeds, he did, it did not affect his health and wellbeing, which shows that he was going through these fasts and personal austerity with sufficient prudence[13]. He lived abstinence with great balance; his purpose was not to hurt himself. As a result, he respected his body as a temple of the Holy Spirit, consecrated on the day of his baptism.

He also was deeply taken by his love of Christ, so he knew that «human beings live not on bread alone» nor on material wealth «but on every word that comes from the mouth of God» (Matthew 4: 4). Father Charbel was sincere in implanting these austerities; every desire of renunciation rose from his heart. The Holy Spirit, who reigned above his soul, made him prosper in sainthood by adopting this lifestyle. This is why Charbel lived his hard life with simplicity, honesty and loyalty.

The Saint of Annaya was also known for his justice. By his justice, he gave his due to God and to his "neighbor"[14]. He adored God in the best way he could. In the monastery and the

---

[13] B. SFEIR, *Ruhaniat Al Keddis Charbel. Chahadat. Taamoulat. Omsulat. Al Jezee Al Sani. Hayatihi el Dayria. Dikatihi fi Hifzi el Kawanin. Fadailihi el Ilahia wal Adabia*, Saint Anthony's Monastery, Lebanon-Ghazir 1996, p 185.
[14] Catechism of the Catholic Church, number 1807.

hermitage, he constantly tried to live an authentic Christian life. Whether during the Holy Mass, the daily communal prayers or his personal ones, Charbel consistently tried to live in communion with the Lord.

A lot can be said about him focusing much more on his duties rather than on his rights. Charbel had no enmities or hostilities. If any misunderstanding occurred, he sincerely tried not to leave any residue of hatred inside his heart. No one reported, from the collected testimonies, that Father Charbel had ever hurt someone with words or attitude. He simply lived his monastic life, trying to fulfill his duties, aiming everything towards the salvation of his soul. He did not want to wait the eternal life in order to live and stay with the Lord, he had already started to live it here on earth, in the heart of the Holy Trinity, through his continuous conversion and prayer.

## 8. *Conviction and Courage*

Father Charbel had a high level of self-contentment. He was truly satisfied with the few things he used to get and was fully aware that every earthly sacrifice will be rewarded in the eternal life. In the hermitage, he ate once a day. The meal did not include any meat, sweets, fruit or wine. Charbel only ate grains, beans, vegetables and bread, he also never smoked or drank coffee. Despite his dedicated work in the vineyard for the twenty-three-year residency, he never tasted the grapes or the wine produced[15]. If the Superior General visited the monastery of Annnaya and a feast was held, Charbel asked the permission not to join them for mealtime.

In addition, Father Charbel never wore new clothes. He preferred to wear old clean clothes rather than new clothes. He used to sleep on a very hard mattress made of animal hair and his pillow consisted of a little piece of wood covered with an old piece of fabric. Several monks at the time had the habit of praying till dawn and Father Charbel also woke up often in prayer.

Courage was also a moral virtue that Charbel had. Courage helps against depression, laziness and drives humans to deal with the difficulties of life. The persistent hermit had been authentic in his courage. He never left the icy winter discourage him. His pleasure was not in torturing himself but in finding God everywhere. Charbel was profoundly convinced that his deeds would bring greater joy and peace. Charbel

---

[15] B. Sfeir, *Ruhaniat Al Keddis Charbel. Chahadat. Taamoulat. Omsulat. Al Jezee Al Sani. Hayatihi el Dayria. Dikatihi fi Hifzi el Kawanin. Fadailihi el Ilahia wal Adabia*, Saint Anthony's Monastery, Lebanon-Ghazir 1996, p 184.

worked and kept hold of an eremitic life from 1875 until 1898.

## 9. *The Silence of the Hermitage*

Since the foundation of the Lebanese Maronite Order, a rule regarding hermits was incorporated in the second part of chapter 13 of the "Book of Regulations". Furthermore, in 1810, the Vicar General Father Ignatius Blaibil added 13 articles as an extension for the original regulations. Based on these articles Saint Charbel lived twenty-three years of his life in Saint Peter and Paul's Hermitage[16]. In accordance with these regulations, Charbel knew that «he did not chose solitude to escape from the rules and monastic commitments». He was looking for virtue and abstinence. He also sought every work that did not contradict silence and reverence for the Lord, as the articles stated. Any useless discussion between monks was forbidden, unless one of them got sick, in this case, they would talk to him with a useful conversation for his wellbeing.

Respecting the regulations of life in the hermitage, Charbel never ate his one daily meal with another person. He did not leave any food or

---

[16] UNIVERSITY OF THE HOLY SPIRIT, *Al Keddis Charbel Makhlouf. Al Raheb Al Lubnani. Salat Al Masa Wal Sabah Wal Kouddas Wal Ziah*, Lebanon-Kaslik 1977, p.50.

drink in his room except for water, which was allowed so the hermit does not get distracted every time he was thirsty. His room was also well isolated, so the crying, the sighing or the singing during prayers could not be heard by the other hermits[17]. The hermit should always remain his solitude unless there were serious and urgent matters. Charbel respected all this until the end of his life.

Other severe canonical rules were also highly observed by Father Charbel. He had to ask for his Superior's permission if he ever decided to wear a hair shirt, thorny metal or anything that might affect his health. Women were not allowed to go into the enclosure of the hermit and if they wanted to participate in the Holy Mass, they knew they should never enter the chapel of the hermitage but remain behind the grate of the exterior chapel door.[18]

## 10. The Long Journey

After twenty-three years passed in silence and calmness since Father Charbel moved to Saint Peter and Paul's Hermitage, he is now seventy

---

[17] P. DAHER, *Saint Charbel*, Saint Maroun's Monastery, Lebanon-Annaya 2012³, p. 131.
[18] P. DAHER, *Saint Charbel*, Saint Maroun's Monastery, Lebanon-Annaya 2012³, p. 133.

years old... He had a long white beard with long white hair which was allowed for hermits as a sign of consecration. His face shined radiantly because it reflected his deep spiritual life. The inner glowing light, that started to shine in him since the novitiate, is now a great blazing flame. Charbel was totally taken by God's presence. He was an old man but continued to obey his superiors. His virtues and his love for Christ were his compass to the heart of the Savior.

During those long years of eremitic life, Father Charbel rarely left the hermitage unless at the request of the Superior General. One time, Patriarch Paul Massaad asked the Superior General of the Order to possibly send the hermit Charbel to the village of Ghadressin Ftouh-Keserwan region in order to bless the sons of the Mr Salloum Al-Dahdah. Salloum had five boys; three of them died from tuberculosis while the other two were still suffering of that calamitous disease. Father Charbel humbly accepted to leave the solitude of the «Hill of Transfiguration» and went to the Salloum's family. Upon his arrival, he blessed the children and stayed there for around a month until the two boys were healed. On his return to the hermitage, a fellow brother asked him about his trip. Charbel kindly responded with a few words, trying as much as possible not to break the silence of hermits.

Charbel looked back at all the years he had spent serving the Lord Jesus. During those years, he was once asked to bless Mr Jibrayil Saba, a disturbed man from the village of Ehmej[19]. Jybrayil had become a threat to himself and others and that is why the inhabitants of Ehmej decided to bring him to the Hermitage in Annaya. When they arrived, it was hard to make him enter the chapel. Consequently, they called Father Charbel to join them out. When the peaceful Charbel arrived, he asked Jibrayil to kneel and cross his hands. He strangely obeyed! Then, Father Charbel took the Gospel book and started to read the Word of God. When he finished, Jibrayil went back to his village in peace, got married and never had another episode of madness for the rest of his life.

In 1885, locusts invaded Mount Lebanon resulting in an agricultural disaster. The Superior General asked Father Charbel to bless some water so the peasants could sprinkle the fields with it. The Hermit Father blessed some water and they sprinkled it all over Annaya's fields. The fields were miraculously saved from locusts. Having heard that story, hundreds of men and women overcrowded the hermitage, asking Father Charbel to bless some water for them so that they could also sprinkle it on their fields. After sprinkling the blessed water, their fields were also

---

[19] *Op. cit.*, p. 155.

saved. A few months later, all the men and women from the surrounding area came to help the monks in the harvest of their land as a sign of gratitude to Father Charbel.

# CHAPTER FOUR

## TOWARDS HEAVEN (1898 - NOWADAYS)

*«LORD, who may abide in your tent?*
*Who shall live on your holy mountain?*

*He who walks blamelessly and does justice;*
*who thinks the truth in his heart*
*and slanders not with his tongue.*

*Who harms not his fellow man,*
*nor takes up a reproach against his neighbor;*
*By whom the reprobate is despised,*
*while he honors those who fear the LORD.*

*Who lends not his money at usury*
*and accepts no bribe against the innocent.*
*He who does these things*
*shall never be disturbed».*

**Psalm 15**

## *1. United With Christ*

In 1898, Charbel's virtues were sharper than ever, he was poor in spirit, gentle, hungry and thirsty for righteousness, merciful and pure of heart. He is to receive what our Lord Jesus promised: «Blessed are the poor in spirit, for theirs is the kingdom of heaven. Blessed are they who mourn, for they will be comforted. Blessed are the meek, for they will inherit the land. Blessed are they who hunger and thirst for righteousness, for they will be satisfied. Blessed are the merciful, for they will be shown mercy. Blessed are the clean of heart, for they will see God. Blessed are the peacemakers, for they will be called children of God. Blessed are they who are persecuted for the sake of righteousness, for theirs is the kingdom of heaven» (Matthew 5: 3-10).

Charbel did not do anything particularly extraordinary or miraculous during his lifetime.

He lived a Christian monastic life, remaining on the Golgotha when he was suffering through the icy winters and the demanding hard work. He accepted to be an apprentice in the school of Jesus Christ. He mainly learned how to give his life without asking for anything in return. For years, he did not speak unless when it was truly necessary. His sense of humility and simplicity became deeply rooted in him and never stopped prospering and flourishing. He became authentically united with Christ, as Saint Paul said: «I live, no longer I, but Christ lives in me» (Galatians 2: 20). He became like John the Baptist «a man who was sent from God. He came for testimony, to testify to the Light, so that all might believe through him. He was not the Light but came to testify to the Light» (John 1: 6-8).

## 2. *His Last Mass*

In December 1898, the monks started preparing for Christmas. Strong storms were hitting the region of Annaya with a lot of rain showers, hail and snow. The temperature was very cold. Inside the walls of the hermitage Father Charbel was no regular hermit, the eremitic life had now deeply embodied his being. The temptations can no longer distress him. He was fulfilled with charity; his heart was fully dedicated to the Lord and no one could take that away.

On the sixteenth of that month, while the old Charbel was celebrating Holy Mass he felt a sudden pain in his body[1]. Father Charbel was seventy years old. For thirty-nine years, he had always celebrated Holy Mass at noon, making the Eucharistic celebration the focus of his day. The winds were icy and the chapel was freezing. A fellow hermit, Father Makarios, noticed that Father Charbel was not feeling well, so he helped him rest a little bit. Shortly afterwards, Father Charbel nodded his head communicating to Father Makarios that he wished to continue. The latter helped him go back to the altar. When Father Charbel was raising the Host and Chalice to say Saint Jacob of Serugh's prayer: «Father of Truth...»[2], he fell down and the monks carried him to his cell. He was hit with paralysis![3]

Annaya's hermit stayed eight days in his cell repeating the Syriac «Father of Truth» (*Abo*

---

[1] S. GAROFALO, *Il Profumo del Libano*, Postulazione Generale dell'Ordine Libanese Maronita, Italia-Roma 2013⁴, p. 232.
[2] S. GAROFALO, *Il Profumo del Libano*, Postulazione Generale dell'Ordine Libanese Maronita, Italia-Roma 2013⁴, p. 233.
[3] M. HAYEK, *Tarik Al Sahraa. Al Abb Charbel, Rahib Min Al Charek: 1828-1898*, Editions Xavier Mappus, France-Le Puy 2013, p. 155.

*Dkoushto*) with great difficulty: «Father of Truth, behold your Son, a willing victim, striving to please you. Condescend to accept Him, for He suffered death so that my existence might be justified. Here is the offering. Take it from my hands with kindness and forget the mistakes I have committed in the presence of Your Divine Majesty. Here is the offering. Here is the blood spilt on Golgotha so that I may attain salvation. He is crying out on my behalf. Consider His merit and accept my contribution. My sins are many, but Your benevolence is great. If You put them together, you will see how Yours outweighs the others, as do the mountains which dominate their surroundings. Consider our sins but take into account also the sacrifice offered for their expiation. The sacrifice and the victim infinitely surpass the mistakes. Because I have sinned, Your Loved One endured the nails and the lance, and His sufferings must surely suffice to satisfy you and give me life».

### 3. *Charbel's Death*

Doctor Najib El Khoury came to examine Father Charbel and asked to give him some soup with meat. Charbel refused eating meat to stay faithful to the eremitic rule. However, when the

Superior of the hermitage asked him, he obeyed[4]. On 24th December 1898, Christmas Eve, Father Charbel peacefully surrendered his soul to God while he was still repeating the Syriac «Father of Truth» and entering the eternal life. It happened in the presence of Father Mikhael Abi Ramia, Father Makarios and Father Boutros Mechmech. Father Mikhael testified later, that he was the last one to give the blessing to Father Charbel, since Father Makarios was very sad to see Father Charbel dying and therefore he could not give him the blessing[5].

On the day of Charbel's death, it was snowing very hard and the snow had blocked the road of the hermitage. The monks were not sure if they were able to transport his body to the cemetery. However, the monks of the monastery of Saint Maroun with the help of some men opened the road with shovels and reached the hermitage. One of the young men while praying in the chapel of the hermitage said: «How is it possible for Father Charbel to stay for twenty three years in this icy place?».

---

[4] S. GAROFALO, *Il Profumo del Libano*, Postulazione Generale dell'Ordine Libanese Maronita, Italia-Roma 2013[4], p. 236.
[5] P. DAHER, *Saint Charbel*, Saint Maroun's Monastery, Lebanon-Annaya 2012[3], p. 168.

When the men and monks finished praying for Father Charbel, they put his body on a bier and went down the road to the monastery. On that bier, Father Charbel rested in peace after his beautiful long journey. The cold wind was blowing through his long white beard, and his fingers were crossed on the praying beads. He was now in the Other World, the world of peace and joy. The monks were singing the ancient Syriac hymns while one of them was leading the procession and incensing the body[6]. On both sides of the road, a few women dressed in black were praying and waiting to see Father Charbel for the last time. For a whole day, the body was left in the church of Saint Maroun's monastery. One by one, Annaya's inhabitants came and took a last look at the Holy Hermit.

However, what God had prepared for Father Charbel was only at its beginning. On the night of the 25th of December, a monk from the monastery went to the chapel for midnight prayer. While he was sitting in the chapel where Father Charbel's body was still exposed, he suddenly saw an extraordinary light flowing out of the tabernacle, reaching the Saint hermit's body and turning up and back to the tabernacle! He immediately ran and called a fellow monk, but when they were together in the chapel, they saw

---

[6] *Op. cit.*, p. 9.

nothing. As a result, the latter monk doubted his vision and asked him skeptical questions. On the morning of 26th December, the body of Father Charbel was buried in the monastery's cemetery[7]. The Holy Hermit's coffin was placed on a piece of wood with several rocks underneath it to prevent water from covering the body, since the cemetery had at the time water leaking problems[8].

## 4. *The Great Light*

«Then Jesus said: "You are the light of the world. A city set on a mountain cannot be hidden. Nor do they light a lamp and then put it under a bushel basket; it is set on a lampstand, where it gives light to all in the house. Just so, your light must shine before others, that they may see your good deeds and glorify your heavenly Father"» (Matthew 5: 14-16).

The first night after Charbel's burial, some peasants ran to the monastery and knocked hard on the door... A monk went straight to the door, opened and asked: «What is going on?!». They responded: «We saw a light coming out of Father Charbel's tomb... floating around the monastery... stopping on the cells and the

---

[7] *Op. cit.*, p. 15.
[8] M. AWAD, *Baraka Ann Kabr Al Keddis Charbel*, Saint Maroun's Monastery, Lebanon-Annaya 2011[3], p. 44.

windows of the church... and finally coming back to the tomb...». The monks did not believe the peasants and thought they were hallucinating.

A week after the funeral, Father Antonious Meshmeshani, the Superior of the monastery came back to Annaya. He felt great grief at Charbel's death. He was very sad for not being able to be present at Charbel's funeral since he desired the Holy Hermit's blessing before his death. Upon his arrival, he went straight to the cemetery, kneeled and prayed for thirty minutes at Charbel's tomb. The monks thought that he was praying for the salvation of the Hermit's soul, but he was praying for Charbel's intercession, asking his blessings for the monastery and the congregation. When he had finished praying, he rose up in sadness and said to the monks gathered there: «We have lost Father Charbel... the spear that was defending our order, our church and our country because of a fatal lightning. Therefore, we must ask God to have mercy on us and give us the grace so the mission of his servant Charbel continues on earth through his corpse present with us. For God had promised the house of David that he will never turn off its lamp on earth for the sake of his servant»[9].

---

[9] M. AWAD, *Baraka Ann Kabr Al Keddis Charbel*, Saint Maroun's Monastery, Lebanon-Annaya 2011³, p. 49.

After this emotional speech, Father Antonious went to his room, closed the door and wrote in the archive of the monastery: «On the twenty fourth of December, year 1898. Father Charbel, a hermit born in Bekaakafra died stricken by paralysis. He was buried in the cemetery of the monastery during Father Antonious Mishmishani's tenure. What this monk will do after his death, will be enough to testify his goodness especially his faithfulness to the vows. His obedience can be described not as human but as angelic»[10]. This authentic prophecy remained unknown by the public until 1950 when the Maronite Patriarch Antoun Boutros Arida asked to exhume Father Charbel's body.

But back to 1898, the light coming out of the Holy Hermit's tomb continued for a month and a half. The Superior was informed every night about what was happening. Crowds gathered every night near the monastery, at the peasants' houses to witness the light. Many Shiite Muslims, living in nearby villages of Byblos were also present and witnessed this light. Because of this, Father Antonious Mishmishani asked the peasants to fire from a hunting rifle when they notice the light so the monks could join them in their houses and see the light. The monks and people saw the

---

[10] P. DAHER, *Charbel. Insan Sekran Bi Allah*, Saint Maroun's Monastery, Lebanon-Annaya 1978², p. 10.

light for several nights and they all agreed that what was happening was far beyond any natural phenomenon!

On one of those evenings, Father Antonious asked one of Annaya's monks, Brother Boutros from Mishmish, to take a pitcher and his lamp to bring water from the source near the monastery's cemetery. Brother Boutros stayed at the water source for twenty minutes while it usually takes only few minutes. At that point, Father Antonious went to the eastern part of the monastery and opened the window to see where Brother Boutros was. He saw him sitting on the ground, with his lamp turned off, the pitcher in his hand and strongly shaking in shock. Brother Boutros told the Superior that night: «I saw Father Charbel like a great shining planet... I saw a flame of fire like a globe with different colors shining out of the grave's door... My lamp turned off and I was unable to return».

On a dark January night, Muslim Ottoman soldiers also noticed the dazzling light around the monastery while searching for a fugitive. The soldiers went to the monastery and investigated the phenomenon. The monks with the Superior told them about all what was going on. Other events related to this phenomenon of the light happened during the first weeks after Father Charbel's death and all the events were written in the monastery's archive[11]. The little glowing light of charity and faith that grew in Charbel's heart was now a dazzling planet that could not be hidden nor could be turned off by his physical death.

## 5. Hiding the Body

As the news of this miraculous light spread, more people from the surrounding region insisted for weeks that Father Antonious Mishmishani open Father Charbel's tomb to examine whether his body was corrupted or not. For that reason, Father Antonious decided to open the tomb and found out that Father Charbel's body was totally incorrupt two months after his death.

Father Antonious went to the Maronite Patriarch Boutros El Howayek and explained to him what was happening and since the incorrupt body showed certain signs of sainthood, Antonious asked the Patriarch the permission to move Father Charbel's body inside the monastery. However, the Patriarch refused to grant him the permission to do so. He asked the Superior of the monastery to keep Father Charbel's body where it must be and make sure that no water or humidity leaks to it. As good servants of the church, the monks did exactly what the Head of their Church

---

[11] M. AWAD, *Baraka Ann Kabr Al Keddis Charbel*, Saint Maroun's Monastery, Lebanon-Annaya 2011$^3$, p. 54.

asked. In the following weeks, the Patriarch came to realize that it was too dangerous to leave the body of a holy man in an open place where anyone could come and steal it. So he gave the permission to open the tomb to protect the body from being stolen. He also asked the monks to put the body somewhere hidden, so the people do not dishonor it in any improper way.

Therefore, the body was taken on the 1st of April 1899 out of the grave. Three months after his death, the body was still sweating and bleeding! For that, they put it in a wooden coffin and left it for a whole day inside the monastery under the sun, so it dries. The next day, they put the coffin in a hidden place inside the northern wall of the church[12] inside the monastery's seclusion making it very hard for men and women to search for it.

When they opened the grave, a Doctor named Saba Bou Mousi, who was suffering from serious backache, decided to visit Father Charbel's tomb. He used to live near Saint Maroun's monastery and had heard about the Holy Hermit's virtues. His back pain started when a lightning hit his house a couple of years before Charbel's death. He tried different treatments but none of them worked and if he ever walked for

---

[12] M. AWAD, *Baraka Ann Kabr Al Keddis Charbel*, Saint Maroun's Monastery, Lebanon-Annaya 2011³, p. 66.

two hours, he had to rest for two days. When the tomb was opened, Saba asked the Superior's permission to be the first one to enter the grave. When he entered, he put his hand on Charbel's body and then rubbed his back. Saba was healed and never had any other health problems!

## 6. *An Incorrupt Body*

Since the beginning of the Church, the incorrupt body of a dead person was considered as a sign of sainthood. It was a divine symbol for the Church, indicating that the person is living the incorrupt and eternal life of heaven. Father Charbel's body, several months after his death, was still very soft and tender as if he was still alive. For that reason, when the monks hid Father Charbel's body in the northern wall, they assigned Father Youssef El Kfoury to take care of it.

Father Youssef, now responsible for the body, took it every night to the rooftop thinking that the eastern hot wind and the morning summer sun would dry it. However, he did this for five months without being able to stop the sweating and bleeding. Eventually, Father Youssef had enough of taking the body out to dry, without any results. He called Doctor Saba Bou Moussi and convinced him after a long discussion to secretly take out the internal organs from the body. The

Superior of the monastery was not there during that period and was not asked for permission. Father Youssef thought that the inner organs of Father Charbel's body were ejecting water and blood and by taking them out, the bleeding and sweating would stop. When they took out the organs, they found them in great condition as if they were taken from a living man. Eventually they buried the internal organs of Father Charbel near the wall of the ruined Saint George's church, fifty meters away from the monastery. Nevertheless, water and blood continued to flow out of the body![13]

When the Superior came back, Father Youssef told him about what he had done, and several investigations were made. The internal organs of Father Charbel were never found again. When the monks dug back to take them out of the box in which they were buried the organs had disappeared[14]. The unstoppable phenomenon of sweating and bleeding continued for many

---

[13] M. AWAD, *Baraka Ann Kabr Al Keddis Charbel*, Saint Maroun's Monastery, Lebanon-Annaya 2011³, p. 97.

[14] Some people say that Doctor Tannous might have taken these organs and used them to heal a lot of his patients. As he did once by taking blood from Father Charbel's body and healed some people by putting a little of it in his medical potions. (Cf. MANSOUR AWAD, *Baraka Ann Kabr Al Keddis Charbel*, Saint Maroun's Monastery, Lebanon-Annaya 2011³, p. 104).

decades. People from every Lebanese village and city arrived and asked for Father Charbel's intercession. Men kneeled on the stairs that led to the place where the body was buried. Women kissed the northern wall of the church when they knew that Charbel's body was buried in the wall. Children laid their heads on that wall. Everybody needed the Holy Hermit's blessings.

A man once brought his mute child and insisted with the monks to let him pray with his child near the body. When the monks finally agreed, he and his child went up the stairs and prayed. Going back home, the child slipped and talked despite being mute! He said: «Father please take my hand». His father looked to the sky and said: «Thank you. O Saint Charbel!». Every single person that came to the monastery asked to go near the tomb. However, the monks continuously said that they should respect the Patriarch's decision and keep people away from the body.

## 7. *Exhumations and Miracles*

In May 1901, various crowds of believers from all over the country arrived to Annaya insisting to see the body of Father Charbel and to pray in front of his tomb. A paralyzed woman was healed after hearing from a Muslim woman that a

Saint was operating miracles in Annaya. A child rose from death, having been given a glass of water blessed by the holy body[15]! Young men regained their sight and several people were liberated from chronic diseases.

Women insisted with tears to see the body of the «Holy Hermit». A lot of people had made long trips to get to Annaya and the monks could not but allow some of the people to see the body during that time. When people saw the body in its incorrupt condition, they were comforted. Furthermore, the sweat and blood that came out of the monk's body during the last three years infiltrated the wall and risked the possibility of revealing where the body was being concealed from pilgrims. Therefore, the Lebanese Maronite Order's General Superior asked the Patriarch's permission to expose the body in a public place, promising that he will prevent people from becoming too attached to this priest.

The monks put the Holy Hermit's body standing upright, in a closet with a glass door, inside a room which was used to receive guests. Father Youssef El Kfoury thought it might be the best way to stop changing the clothes on the body twice a week. That room was only opened for

---

[15] H. ISKANDAR, *Saint Charbel From His Contemporaries To Our Era*, Hawk Network Corporation, Lebanon-Antelias 2013, p. 68.

Holy Mass or when pilgrims were at the monastery. During those years, the arriving pilgrims saw the Holy Hermit on his feet, standing in the closet, praying with them and for them; he had his head bending to the right, his eyes closed, and his white moustache, beard and hair were still intact since his death[16].

In 1907, the Apostolic Visitators, nominated by the Holy See to canonically visit the Maronite Orders asked the Superior of the monastery to put the body in a coffin which was more dignified for a deceased monk. Therefore, the monks put the body back into a coffin which remained closed until 24th July 1927 when the tomb was opened to examine the body. On that day, twenty-nine years after his death, Father Charbel's body was still bleeding and sweating![17]

Four doctors examined the body in 1910 and said that the bleeding and the sweating were surely extraordinary and unusual. A famous Pharmacist and Doctor, Georges Antoun Chikrallah, examined the body thirty six times between 1908 and 1926, always finding it in the same incorrupt condition. He also paid for a very expensive coffin in 1908 to put the body in, since

---

[16] M. AWAD, *Baraka Ann Kabr Al Keddis Charbel*, Saint Maroun's Monastery, Lebanon-Annaya 2011³, p. 113.
[17] *Op. cit.*, p. 107.

he noticed the miserable condition of the coffin in which Father Charbel was placed.

However, not all doctors were as convinced as Doctor Chikrallah. In fact, a Doctor Najib Bek El Khoury once asked the monks to put lime under the feet of Charbel saying that this white material will absorb all the blood and water coming out of the body. But when he turned back several months later, he was astonished to see the body always in good condition despite putting lime under it, and confessed that his true intention was to ruin the body with that lime, but he did not succeed![18]

In 1925, Father Ignatius El Tannoury, the Superior General of the Lebanese Maronite Order went to Rome and asked Pope Pius XI to start the beatification process for Father Charbel Makhlouf, along with Father Nimatullah Kassab, Charbel's teacher at Kfifan, and Sister Rafqa Ar-Rayès. The Pope agreed and a canonical committee was established in May 1926 and started its investigations[19]. On 22nd February 1950, the tomb was opened again to examine the body. That year was called the «Holy Year», for literally thousands of miracles were operated by

---

[18] M. AWAD, *Baraka Ann Kabr Al Keddis Charbel*, Saint Maroun's Monastery, Lebanon-Annaya 2011³, p. 122.
[19] P. DAHER, *Saint Charbel*, Saint Maroun's Monastery, Lebanon-Annaya 2012³, p. 28.

Father Charbel. Several other exhumations were done: on 22nd August 1952, the body was left for two weeks in a coffin made of Cedar wood sealed with a glass on its top so the crowds could pass and receive a blessing. On 2nd April 1955, the Holy See asked to open the tomb to examine it during the beatification process. On that day, fifty-seven years after his death the body was still in a very good condition and still bleeding and sweating! In 1965, the tomb was opened once again to take relics for the beatification day and the body was found as usual in an excellent state, still bleeding! His clothes and the coffin were musty, but his body always had a wonderful smell[20], "the aroma of Christ" (2 Corinthians 2:15).

## 8. *Thousands of Miracles*

When Jesus Christ was preaching in Israel, John the Baptist heard in prison of the works of the Messiah, so he sent his disciples to him with this question: «"Are you the one who is to come, or should we look for another?" Jesus said to them in reply: "Go and tell John what you hear and see: the blind regain their sight, the lame walk, lepers are cleansed, the deaf hear, the dead

---

[20] P. DAHER, *Charbel. Insan Sekran Bi Allah*, Saint Maroun's Monastery, Lebanon-Annaya 1978², p. 26.

are raised, and the poor have the good news proclaimed to them. And blessed is the one who takes no offense with me". As they were going off, Jesus began to speak to the crowds about John: "What did you go out to the desert to see? A reed swayed by the wind? Then what did you go out to see? Someone dressed in fine clothing? Those who wear fine clothing are in royal palaces. Then why did you go out? To see a prophet? Yes, I tell you, and more than a prophet"» (Matthew 11: 2-9).

During the 1950s, the humble hermit of Annaya appeared and performed miracles all over the world. Father Charbel's miracles were witnessed and written about in journals of Iraq, Brazil, Egypt, Syria, United States of America, Australia, Argentina, France, Belgium, Malta...[21] Thousands of men and women from all over the world started arriving to Annaya to visit Father Charbel's shrine.

In 1950, Emile Lahoud, Lebanese Minister of Finance at that time, could not believe what was happening at Annaya. He went to the Lebanese Presidential Palace and protested in front of Bechara El Khoury, the President of the Lebanese Republic, to stop this «nonsense». The

---

[21] H. ISKANDAR, *Saint Charbel From His Contemporaries To Our Era*, Hawk Network Corporation, Lebanon-Antelias 2013, p. 80.

Lebanese President asked him to go to Annaya and figure out what was truly going on. Upon his arrival to the monastery, the Superior was pleased to welcome him. Minister Lahoud immediately said that he did not believe what was happening there, therefore he wished to see with his own eyes. While sitting at the Superior's office, they heard people applauding and people shouting: «A miracle… A miracle…»! The Minister panicked and went out of the office. He suddenly saw his mentally disturbed neighbor Akl Wakim acting normally. The Minister's neighbor had suffered madness and had abnormal episodes and behaviors for fifteen years. The Minister checked out his neighbor many times and ended by certifying the miracle. The Minister believed and eventually asked to write about the miracle with his own hand in the monastery's archive. When the Archivist noticed that he signed without writing his title of Deputy and Minister, he asked him to add it, but the Minister refused stating: «Here, in front of the greatness of Charbel, everything bows down»[22].

In that same year, the leg and back nerves of an Iraqi child were also healed. Victor Kimawy, a man from Sao Paulo Brazil was cured from heart disease. A young Egyptian Muslim girl

---

[22] P. DAHER, *Saint Charbel*, Saint Maroun's Monastery, Lebanon-Annaya 2012³, p. 35.

called Amal Ali, was cured from typhoid after being anointed with oil brought by her father from Charbel's shrine. A little Syrian girl named Yvonne Khoury hit by typhoid that deformed her hip leaving her lame, was relieved from illness after visiting the monk's tomb. Salim Ghantous, a man from Florida in the United States of America was sick with diabetes and subject to serious high blood sugar levels that might have led to his death was healed after asking for Father Charbel's intercession. Joseph Antoun, a man from Sydney Australia came with a walking disability and returned with his full strength after asking for the Lebanese monk's intercession. Several Argentinian newspapers wrote on their front pages about a pilot called Edwardo Muraria who was staying in a hotel called Saint Charbel at Noken city. While leaving, Edwardo asked the reason for the hotel's name, he was told that the owners were Lebanese citizens and they named the hotel after a very famous Lebanese saint. On that day, Edwardo had to fly a small airplane whose engine suddenly stopped. He started shouting: «Saint Charbel save us!». Even though the airplane crashed to the ground, all the passengers miraculously survived without any injuries. The pilot said in several interviews that it was the first airplane crash with no casualties!

In 1957, the French journal "Içi Paris", wrote the story of a woman healed of paralysis and gained the power to walk again "like a reindeer" after asking Father Charbel's intercession! After publishing this story, hundreds of sick and ill French people were cured after asking for Father Charbel's intercession. A French woman was cured of cancer after being blessed by a little piece of cloth from the Holy Hermit's tomb. Another woman who was sick with terminal kidney problems after giving birth was cured by Father Charbel Makhlouf.[23]

In less than two years, between 1950 and 1952, Annaya's monastery received more than 135,000 letters from 95 different countries, thanking God and Father Charbel for their healing or asking for a little piece of cloth blessed by his tomb. The monks responded as much as they could to these letters[24]. Every person who visited Lebanon asked how to get to Annaya. Lebanon was no more known because it was mentioned 75 times in the Bible or for its fascinating history, archeological sites or beautiful nature but for its precious Father Charbel Makhlouf from Annaya.

---

[23] H. ISKANDAR, *Al Keddis Charbel Mn Mouasirih Ila Asrina*, Our Lady of Al Qalaa, Lebanon-Menjez 2009, p. 181.
[24] P. DAHER, *Saint Charbel*, Saint Maroun's Monastery, Lebanon-Annaya 2012³, p. 36.

## 9. Blessed Charbel Makhlouf

Saint Peter once said to the Lord Jesus: «"We have given up everything and followed you. What will there be for us?" Jesus said to them: "Amen, I say to you that you who have followed me, when everything is made new again, when the Son of Man is seated on his throne of glory, will yourselves sit on twelve thrones, judging the twelve tribes of Israel. And everyone who has given up houses or brothers or sisters or father or mother or children or lands for the sake of my name will receive a hundred times more, and will inherit eternal life"» (Matthew 19: 27-29).

On 5th December 1965, Pope Paul VI declared Charbel Makhlouf as "Blessed" in Saint Peter's Basilica at the Vatican on the closure of the Second Vatican Council. A convoy of the highest Lebanese politicians and ecclesiastic figures were present for the ceremony. In addition, thousands of Catholic bishops from all over the world who were present at the Vatican for the Ecumenical Council also participated in the beatification celebrations. Charbel had inherited the eternal life and this reality can no longer be hidden.

From the thousands of extraordinary miracles performed by the Saint of Annaya, two were significantly important and particularly considered to proceed in the canonization. The first miracle was the curing of Sister Mary Abel from the congregation of the Holy Hearts of Jesus and Mary. Sister Mary was suffering from pain in the abdomen and could not bear to eat any food whatsoever. She ended up vomiting whatever she ate[25]. She suffered for fourteen years and tried every possible cure without any success. She ended by losing all her strength, was unable to walk and therefore was constantly carried by others. Eventually, after hearing about Father Charbel's miracles, she prayed to him and said: «If you want to heal me, let me see you while I am sleeping». On that night, she saw Father Charbel in a dream. He was near her bed standing with his hand over her! She also saw him on another night, kneeling and blessing her. Consequently, on 11th July 1950, she went to Saint Maroun's monastery. Upon her arrival, she put her hand on the Saint's tomb. She suddenly felt like an electric wave passing through her back[26]. After experiencing several events and while praying on the Saint's tomb the day after her arrival, she noticed drops of water coming out of the tomb's door! She took her tissue, wiped up

---

[25] A. CHEBLI, *Al Abb Charbel Makhlouf. Mn Abnaa Al Rahbania Al Baladya Al Lubnania Al Marounia. Habis Mahbasit Deir Annaya*, Saint Maroun Monastery, Lebanon-Annaya 1999², p. 157.
[26] *Op. cit.*, p. 159.

the water and scrubbed the part of her body where it hurt most. She immediately rose to her feet. All the pilgrims present in the monastery started to glorify the Lord for this miracle.

The second miracle occurred with Iskandar Obeid[27], a blacksmith from Baabdat, who had lost sight in one of his eyes during a work accident in 1937. He had tried all possible cures. When Father Charbel's miracles of 1950 started to become famous his neighbors told him to go to Annaya and pray the Holy Hermit. However, he continuously said I will only go when Father Charbel gives me a sign. He prayed for several months waiting for the sign. On a usual night, while sleeping, he saw a monk telling him: «Go to the Monastery and you will be healed». In the morning, Iskandar went to Annaya, participated in Holy Mass and slept there. From the time of his arrival to the shrine, Iskandar started feeling pain in his blinded eye. When he returned to his village, the pain was growing until he could no longer work anymore. A couple of days later, he saw himself in a dream in front of an ancient church dedicated to Saint Moses. He also saw a monk coming to him and asking: «Have you been here for a long time?». Iskandar responded: «I have been here since the morning». The monk

---

[27] P. DAHER, *Saint Charbel*, Saint Maroun's Monastery, Lebanon-Annaya 2012³, p. 187.

said: «Why haven't you told us to come and heal your eye?». The monk then explained that he will put a "powder" in his blinded eye that will cause some pain, but it will surely heal him. He suddenly woke up startled and his wife sleeping by his side immediately woke up. Iskandar started to shout telling his wife: «Bring the photo of Saint Charbel... Hurry up...». He closed the eye in which he sees and opened the blind one to examine if he was seeing. He was miraculously able to see Saint Charbel's photo with his blinded eye! A guest sleeping over at their place woke up, as well and the whole neighborhood, and fled to their house on that night because of Iskandar's shouting. When the neighbors saw the miracle, they glorified the Lord. The same doctors and specialists that have examined his blinded eye were stunned by this miracle.

## 10. Charbel Makhlouf... a Saint

On 9th October 1977, during the Lebanese Civil war, the chaotic sounds of the war were overcome by great harmonious sounds. It was the sound of the canonization of Father Charbel Makhlouf at the Vatican. Every Lebanese communication agency was covering the event. Wounded Lebanon, struggling to get out of war, was filled with joy. The Lebanese people had lived many sorrows during those years, but God had prepared an exceptional joy for them. Bekaakafra's son was being canonized by Pope Paul VI. The monk, priest and hermit was now invading Lebanon with the happiness of his canonization. His miracles have reached every single country on the planet. He was a testimony that: «Nothing is impossible for God» (Luke 1: 37). As if «it was of him that the prophet Isaiah had spoken when he said: "A voice of one crying out in the desert, 'Prepare the way of the Lord, make straight his paths"» (Matthew 3: 3).

On that marvelous day, the Pope delivered a very beautiful Homily in which he said:

«The Church of East and West is invited today to a great joy. Our heart is turned towards heaven, where we certainly know by now that Charbel Makhlouf is associated with the immeasurable happiness of saints, in the light of Christ, praising and interceding for us. […] The turmoil of the recent events (the Lebanese Civil War) have excavated deep wrinkles on his face and left a shadow on the road of peace. However, you know our constant sympathy and affection. […] His lamp turned on the top of his hermitage's mountain, in the last century, has shined with an ever greater brightness and humanity has quickly gathered around his sainthood. […] Let us hear the words of his mother after separating from her: "If you are not going to be a good religious man, I would tell you: Come back home. However, I now know that God wants you at His service. Moreover, in the pain of being separated from you, I confidently tell Him: May He bless you, my child and make you a Saint". [...] What does such a life then represent? The assiduous practice, pushed to the extreme, of the three vows of religion, lived in silence and monastic despoliation: the strict poverty which has to do with housing, clothes, only one frugal daily meal during hard handwork in the rough mountain's weather. A chastity surrounded by a legendary intransigency. Finally and specially, a total obedience to his superiors and even for his fellow brothers and for the eremitic rule that translates his total submission to God. Nevertheless, the key of this life that looks strange in its appearance was the pursuit of sainthood, which means the most perfect conformity to Christ, humble and poor, the uninterrupted conversation with the Lord, the personal participation to the sacrifice of Christ through passionate celebration of the Holy Mass and throw the rigorous penitence joined with the intercession for sinners. [...] Since his death the light had shined furthermore on his tomb: many people, searching for spiritual progress, continue to be fascinated by this man of God [...] Yes, the type of Charbel Makhlouf's sainthood has a great weight, not only for the glory of God but also for the vitality of the Church. [...] May the new Saint continue exercising his prodigious influence, not only in Lebanon, but also in the East and in the whole Church! May he intercede for us, poor sinners that we, very often, do not risk the experience of the beatitude that leads to the perfect joy! May he intercede for his brothers in the Lebanese Maronite Order and for the whole Maronite Church, of which everyone knows its worth and its trials! May he intercede for the dear Lebanon and helps it to overpass the difficulties of the hour, takes care of the wounds that are still alive, and helps it to walk into hope! May he sustain and guides him to the right path, as we just sang! May his light shine over Annaya, allying men in concord and attracting them to God, which he is contemplating by now in the eternal happiness! Amen!»[28]

---

[28] PAUL VI, *Homélie pour la Canonisation de Charbel Makhlouf*, Vatican City, 9 October 1977.

# FINAL REFLECTION AND PRAYER

The little boy of Beqaakafra grew up to become a Saint! His name is now known all over the world. The majority of people from his era are now no longer remembered. However, Charbel's sainthood is now unforgettable. His sainthood has attracted people from all over the world. With Charbel's intercession, every human being can hope to change, can hope to heal. What is hopeless is now hopeful. What is uncontrollable and is now controllable. Annaya's lamp today is a great flame and no wind can blow it out.

«Seek first the kingdom of God and his righteousness, and all these things will be given you besides» (Matthew 6, 33) Jesus said, and this is exactly what Charbel did. Annaya's Saint lived his earthly life as a pilgrim and a stranger, God sent him to heal the broken spirits of His people. 26, 000 miracles are till the date of writing this book registered in Annaya's archive, and it is only the beginning... The hermitage in which very few hermits lived a century ago, is now crowded by hundreds of thousands of pilgrims every year. Charbel always sought the kingdom of God and lived his life, not for himself, but for Christ so that «it is no longer I who live, but Christ who lives within me» (Galatians 2:20). He is now leading people towards Jesus Christ, the goal and fulfilment of life.

> Blessed are you, O peaceful Saint Charbel, for your virtues and your experience with the Lord.
>
> Blessed are you, O silent Saint Charbel, for your deep belief in Mercy.
>
> Blessed are you, O great Saint Charbel, for you are now healer of bodies and souls.
>
> Blessed are you, O wonderful Saint Charbel, for your biography now is the dream that every Christian dares to dream.
>
> Blessed are you, O magnificent Saint Charbel, for you are a guarantee for the mainstream of your Church.
>
> Blessed are you, O beloved Saint Charbel, for becoming a proof that Christ is with us till the end of days.
>
> Blessed are you, O sweet Hermit of Annaya, for you are by now far beyond any earthly inspiration.

## Final Reflection And Prayer

And blessed are you, O tranquil Saint Charbel, for becoming a lamp of Eternal Lights!

# BIBLIOGRAPHY

1. DAHER, P., *Saint Charbel*, Saint Maroun's Monastery, Lebanon-Annaya 2012[3].

2. DE LIGUORI, A., *Preparation for Death*, J.B. Lippincott and co., England-London 1869.

3. GAROFALO, S., *Il Profumo del Libano. San Sciarbel Makhluf. Monaco ed eremita dell'Ordine Libanese Maronita (1828-1898)*, Postulazione Generale dell'Ordine Libanese Maronita, Italia-Roma 2013[4].

4. ISKANDAR, H., *Saint Charbel From His Contemporaries To Our Era*, Hawk Network Corporation, Lebanon-Antelias 2013.

5. PAUL VI, *Homélie pour la Canonisation de Charbel Makhlouf*, Vatican City, 9 october 1977.

6. SAVART, C. (Sous la direction), «Charbel Makhlouf» dans *Histoire des Saints Et De La Sainteté Chrétienne. Vers Une Sainteté Universelle 1715 - à nos jours*, 2ᵉ Partie, Tome X, Hachette, France-Paris 1995, p. 181.

## Books in Arabic (transliterated in Latin letters)

7. ABOU SAMRA, G., *Charbel Ibn Hal Jabal*, Saint Charbel's House, Lebanon-Bekaakafra 2012.

8. AWAD, M., *Baraka Ann Kabr Al Keddis Charbel*, Saint Maroun's Monastery, Lebanon-Annaya 2011[3].

9. CHEBLI, A., *Al Abb Charbel Makhlouf. Mn Abnaa Al Rahbania Al Baladya Al Lubnania Al Marounia. Habis Mahbasit Deir Annaya*, Saint Maroun Monastery, Lebanon-Annaya 1999[2].

10. DAHER, P., *Charbel. Insan Sekran Bi Allah*, Saint Maroun's Monastery, Lebanon-Annaya 1978[2].

11. HAYEK, M., *Tarik Al Sahraa. Al Abb Charbel, Rahib Min Al Charek: 1828-1898*, Editions Xavier Mappus, France-Le Puy 2013.

12. ISKANDAR, H., *Al Keddis Charbel Mn Mouasirih Ila Asrina*, Our Lady of Al Qalaa, Lebanon-Menjez 2009.

13. KHACHAN, Y., *Al Kawakib Al Khamsa*, Lebanese Maronite Order, 1996[3].

14. SAIFI, A., *Chajarit Aaliat Mar Charbel*, Lebanon-Bekaakafra 1990.

15. SFEIR, B., *Ruhaniat Al Keddis Charbel. Chahadat. Taamoulat. Omsulat. Al Jezee Al Awwal. Hadasatahou. Tarahoubahou. Kahanoutahou,*

# BIBLIOGRAPHY

Saint Anthony's Monastery, Lebanon-Ghazir 1995.

**16.** SFEIR, B., *Ruhaniat Al Keddis Charbel. Chahadat. Taamoulat. Omsulat. Al Jezee Al Sani. Hayatihi el Dayria. Dikatihi fi Hifzi el Kawanin. Fadailihi el Ilahia wal Adabia*, Saint Anthony's Monastery, Lebanon-Ghazir 1996.

**17.** SAINT CHARBEL'S FAMILY, *Hayat Al Keddis Charbel*, Lebanon-Zahle 2005.

**18.** UNIVERSITY OF THE HOLY SPIRIT, *Al Keddis Charbel Makhlouf. Al Raheb Al Lubnani. Salat Al Masa Wal Sabah Wal Kouddas Wal Ziah*, Lebanon-Kaslik 1977.

## *From the Vatican's Official website www.vatican.va:*

**19.** Catechism of the Catholic Church:
www.vatican.va/archive/ENG0015/_INDEX.HTM

**20.** Nimatullah Kassab Al-Hardini:
www.vatican.va/news_services/liturgy/saints/ns_lit_doc_20040516_al-hardini_en.html

# INDEX

PREFACE ................................................................. 7
INTRODUCTION ..................................................... 9

## CHAPTER ONE
### From Birth to Early Adulthood (1828-1851) ............. 15
1. The Crying of a Newborn ............................................. 17
2. Beqaakafra ................................................................... 20
3. His Father Leaves ........................................................ 22
4. His Father's Death ....................................................... 24
5. The Grotto ................................................................... 26
6. The Lebanese Maronite Order ..................................... 28
7. Youssef's Uncles ......................................................... 31
8. «A Tiny Whispering Sound» ....................................... 33
9. «Lord, to Whom Whall We Go?» ................................ 34

## CHAPTER TWO
### The Glorious Thunder of a Monk (1851-1875) ......... 37
1. The First Year of the Novitiate .................................... 41
2. «Is Fit for the Kingdom of God» ................................. 43

3. The Novitiate's Life ........................................... 45
　　4. Annaya .............................................................. 48
　　5. The End of the Novitiate ................................... 49
　　6. In Heaven We Shall meet .................................. 51
　　7. Kfifan ............................................................... 53
　　8. Father Nimatullah Kassab .................................. 55
　　9. «Do This in Remembrance of Me» .................... 57

## CHAPTER THREE
## The Eternal Light of a Hermit (1875-1898) ............... 61
　　1. Sixteen Years .................................................... 65
　　2. «The Hill of Transfiguration» ............................ 68
　　3. The Miracle of the Lamp ................................... 70
　　4. Many Battles He Had Won ................................ 73
　　5. His Daily Life in the Hermitage ......................... 75
　　6. His Vows and Theological Virtues ..................... 76
　　7. Prudence and Justice ......................................... 78
　　8. Conviction and Courage .................................... 80
　　9. The Silence of the Hermitage ............................ 82
　　10. The Long Journey ............................................ 83

## CHAPTER FOUR
## Towards Heaven (1898 - nowadays) .......................... 87
　　1. United With Christ ............................................ 89

# INDEX

2. His Last Mass .................................................................. 90
3. Charbel's Death ............................................................. 92
4. The Great Light ............................................................. 95
5. Hiding the Body ............................................................ 99
6. An Incorrupt Body ....................................................... 101
7. Exhumations and Miracles ........................................... 103
8. Thousands of Miracles ................................................. 107
9. Blessed Charbel Makhlouf .......................................... 112
10. Charbel Makhlouf… a Saint ...................................... 115

**FINAL REFLECTION AND PRAYER** ..................... 119

**BIBLIOGRAPHY** ....................................................... 125
**INDEX** ......................................................................... 129

PLEASE CONSIDER
REVIEWING THIS BOOK ON:
*Amazon*


SUBSCRIBE ON ELIAS TURK'S
YOUTUBE CHANNEL:
*A Catholic in Rome*

## THIS BOOK IS AVAILABLE IN FOUR OTHER LANGUAGES ON AMAZON:

1. **IL POTENTE TAUMATURGO**: UNA BIOGRAFIA DI SAN CHARBEL MAKHLOUF (1828 – 1898)

2. **LÁMPARA DE LUZ ETERNA**: BIOGRAFÍA DE SAN CHARBEL MAKHLOUF (1828-1898)

3. **A LUZ ETERNA**: BIOGRAFIA DO SANTO CHARBEL MAKHLOUF (1828-1898)

4. **سراج النور**: سيرة القدّيس شربل مخلوف

---

## ELIAS TURK'S BOOKS:

1. **LAMP OF ETERNAL LIGHTS**: THE BIOGRAPHY OF SAINT CHARBEL MAKHLOUF (1828-1898)

2. **ANDATE DA GIUSEPPE**: 12 LEZIONI DA SAN GIUSEPPE

3. **PADRE PIO**: UNA BREVE BIOGRAFIA (1887-1968)

4. **من الفجر ولدتُكَ**: سيرة القدّيس مكسيميليان ماريّا كولبي

5. **أميرة الفقراء**: سيرة القدّيسة الأميرة أليصابات المجريّة

Made in the USA
Monee, IL
25 July 2025